THE NAUGHTY KID'S HANDBOOK

ROD GREEN

DINO

Published by Dino Books,
an imprint of John Blake Publishing Ltd,
3 Bramber Court, 2 Bramber Road,
London W14 9PB, England

www.johnblakepublishing.co.uk

www.facebook.com/johnblakebooks ◼
twitter.com/jblakebooks ◼

This edition published in paperback in 2015

ISBN: 978 1 78418 338 7

British Library Cataloguing-in-Publication Data:

A catalogue record for this book is available from the British Library.

Design by www.envydesign.co.uk

Printed in Great Britain by CPI Group (UK) Ltd

1 3 5 7 9 10 8 6 4 2

Papers used by John Blake Publishing are natural, recyclable products made
from wood grown in sustainable forests. The manufacturing processes
conform to the environmental regulations of the country of origin.

Every attempt has been made to contact the relevant copyright-holders,
but some were unobtainable. We would be grateful if the appropriate
people could contact us.

Contents

Introduction

So you want to be a Naughty Kid? Well, if you're reading this we have to assume that you either want to be a Naughty Kid or you are a spoil-sport grown-up who has cruelly confiscated this book from some kid who was innocently reading through it with no intention of ever doing anything naughty in his or her entire life. If you are that grown-up, you might as well stop reading now because there is nothing interesting in here whatsoever and you are totally wasting your time. You probably have something far better to do, like hoovering your eyebrows, or complaining to the council about the noise the birds make first thing in the morning. Off you go and make yourself busy!

Right, now that we've got rid of any snoopers, let's get down to the serious naughty business! Before you can truly regard yourself as a Naughty Kid, you have to understand what a Naughty Kid really is. THEY – the grown-ups, parents, teachers and everyone else who's always got it in for you – think that pretty much everything you do is naughty. THEY think you're being naughty if you don't smile at them, say, 'Hello! It's so wonderful to see you', and dance around them like a demented puppy every time they walk into the room. THEY think you're being naughty if you're walking in a relaxed way with your hands in your pockets (okay, maybe a bit of a slouch) instead of marching along with your back ramrod-straight, like some boot-stomping soldier on parade. THEY basically think you're being naughty if you do anything that gets on their nerves – and the list of things that clamber all over their precious nerves is longer and more boring than one of those TV shows that THEY like. You know – the ones about buying antique soup plates to hang on the walls of the house that you're renovating in the countryside and how much more money the house is worth with a soup plate on the wall.

Essentially, THEY know nothing – or do they? Never forget that grown-ups, unlikely as it may seem – were once as young as you. That means that THEY might be aware that you are trying to pull a dodge or a scam, so a true Naughty Kid never underestimates the enemy, always preparing well and practising thoroughly before putting a plan into action. You may well be able to use some of the tips in this book when devising your plans, or you might adapt them to suit your own needs, or you might use them as inspiration to come up with your own cunning schemes for naughty deeds. What sort of things might they be?

Well, we can say for certain what they won't be. Naughty Kids don't go around smashing windows or spraying graffiti on walls. That's not naughty, that's just stupid. You have nothing to gain from that sort of behaviour and Naughty Kids are not stupid. You have to be smart to be a Naughty Kid. The whole point of pulling truly naughty stunts, scams and dodges is that you get something out of it. You are in it to win it – Naughty Kids always aim to come out on top. But you want to be a winner without hurting anyone else, or yourself. Naughty Kids don't put themselves or those around them in any kind of danger. Again, that's not naughty; it's just plain stupid.

What Naughty Kids *do* want to do is duck out of chores, or sports, or being forced to do anything they *don't* want to do. They don't eat stuff they hate or do everything that THEY tell them to – not if there's a way to get out of it.

Naughty Kids also have fun, and that's the most important thing. If your main aim is to have a bit of a laugh, it's much easier for you to flash your most charming smile and make a joke of it all, should a scam go horribly wrong. THEY will only see the funny side of a stunt if you do, and making it all out to be a huge joke is your last line of defence if you land yourself in scalding hot water.

The way to avoid ending up in a deep, deep pit of doo-doo is to develop your talents as a Naughty Kid so that you become an expert in subterfuge. That's a good word: subterfuge. If you look it up, you'll find that it covers deception, intrigue, double-dealing and all of the skills required by a superspy or a top secret agent. Being a successful Naughty Kid is really quite like being a secret agent working undercover. You have to be skilled in disguise, highly proficient in manufacturing the props you will need to pull off your dodges and, most importantly, a master of deception. In other words, you have to be good at telling porkies.

THEY will tell you constantly that you should never tell lies but, if THEY were totally honest, they'd have to admit that THEY have told such whoppers in the past that they ran the risk of growing a nose that would make Pinocchio's look like a puny little pimple.

There's no way round it. If you're going to stage successful Naughty Kid dodges, you'll have to make your fibs sound utterly convincing. That means that you have to know how to tell a lie in such a way that no one would ever suspect you were fibbing, and to do that you have to be able to recognise a good lie from a bad one. You must be able to tell fact from fib. To help you with that, there are three 'Fantastic Fact or Fab Fibs' featured in each section of this book. Only one of the three is actually a real fact ... maybe. You'll have to make up your mind about that yourself, then check the list of Fantastic Facts at the back of the book.

So, if you want to be a Naughty Kid, keep your wits about you at all times, keep yourself and those around you safe, practise your skills, practise your fibbing and – above all else – have a shedload of fun!

How to Make Your Bike Sound Like a Motorbike

So you've been in your room for hours, Skyping, texting, emailing, tweeting, gaming or otherwise communicating with the outside world, when you're suddenly ordered out to 'get a bit of fresh air for a change' or to 'get your bike out and go and talk to your friends instead of shutting yourself away in your room'. How can parents be so stupid? You were already talking to your friends. They've all shut themselves away in their rooms as well, trying to avoid being sent out for 'fresh air'!

Still, your bike is okay. Pity it's not

a motorbike, though. It would be brilliant to go roaring up and down the street on a motorbike – that's a cool noise. But you are way too young to be able to ride a motorbike and your bike doesn't make the sort of noise that will get the neighbours' curtains twitching when they dare to peek out and see what sort of biker has just arrived. Your bike ticks along as silent as a stopped clock. There's no way it could ever sound like a motorbike – or is there?

Kids have been inventing ways to make their bikes sound like motorbikes for years but you now have the means to do it louder than ever before and really shake up the neighbourhood! To explain how, we first have to agree on what various bits of your bike's frame are called so that we all know what we're talking about.

Fantastic Fact or Fab Fib?

Soldiers have been issued with bicycles since the First World War and paratroops being dropped behind enemy lines had the first folding bicycles, which were easy to carry and could be eaten in emergencies.

The frame of your bike is made of tubes (usually steel tubes) and the tubes that hold the rear wheel in place form a kind of a triangle. The two tubes that run from the centre of the rear wheel to where the pedals turn the chain are called the 'chain stays'. These are the base of the triangle. The two tubes that run up from the rear wheel towards the seat are called the 'seat stays'. These form the outer edge of the triangle. The only other bits of the frame that we need concern ourselves with are the two tubes running either side of the front wheel, from the handlebar area down to the centre of the front wheel. These two are called the 'front fork'.

Now, on to the different ways of making that motorbike sound!

The oldest way of making a bike sound as if it's got an engine is to jam an ordinary playing card into the spokes of the front or rear wheel so that it sticks out and slaps against the chain stays, seat stays or, in the case of the front wheel, the front fork, when the wheel is turning. Two or three cards give you more slaps and make a fairly good 'ripping' motorbike sound. Rather than jam the cards in the spokes, try taping them in place on the stays or the front fork so that they are whacked by the spokes as the wheel turns. This also gives a reasonably good noise, but either of these methods eventually suffers from the cards wearing out. It's easy enough to replace them, but what we really want is a bit more volume, and a deeper tone that sounds like a more powerful engine.

One way of achieving this is to use a Coke can. Any empty soft-drink can will do. Lie it on the ground and run over the middle of the can – just once – with your front wheel. You're not riding the bike at this point, just pushing it forwards with your hands on the handlebars, pressing down to put some weight on the front wheel. The two ends of the can will fold upwards as it is crushed and grip onto your wheel. As the wheel rotates, it will bring the can up to the top of the front fork, where the two arms join, and it will sit there behind the fork as the wheel revolves. When you are pedalling along, your knobbly tyre will rub against the can, producing a growly engine sound. Because the can acts like a kind of echo chamber and amplifies the sound, this is a louder, more powerful-sounding engine noise than the playing cards. The main problem is that the can is likely to be dislodged if you go over a bump or if you have to walk your bike backwards for any reason, and once it's off, you can never get it to work as well again.

Fantastic Fact or Fab Fib?

Aztecs raced the first bicycles with wooden wheels around specially-built wheelodromes at Catchimifyoucan in Peru.

Even louder than the can is the small plastic bottle. Remove the cap and crush the bottle as flat as you can, then jam it into the space between the top of the rear wheel and the part of the frame where the two seat stays come together. As you pedal along, your rear tyre will rub against the bottle and make a very convincing engine roar. The noise comes out of the open neck of the bottle, amplified by the bottle in the

same way that the can boosts the noise from the front wheel. The trouble with this method is that it can interfere with your rear brakes and, even though you might not be doing the 150 mph it sounds like you're doing, if you can't stop, you are likely to come a cropper. Remember, if you pull on your front brake when you're going fast, it's not an engine you'll want; it's wings, because you will be flying over the handlebars. If the bottle messes with your rear brakes, then you should go for the final option.

The last, and the loudest, engine noise is also made by an empty plastic bottle, but you need a bigger one this time. You don't have to crush it, so it makes a better echo chamber and an excellent, dirt-bike-style howl. All you have to do is unscrew the cap from the bottle and hold it upside down between the chain stay (on the opposite side from the actual chain) and the rear spokes. It needs to be pushed in between the spokes and the stay, touching both, so that when you wheel the bike forward the bottle is drawn in and jams between the chain stay and the spokes. Obviously it has to be a big enough plastic bottle to wedge itself in there. Now, when you pedal away, you'll be making a noise like a high-powered dirt bike. Of course, this doesn't do your spokes much good, but the bottle will wear out long before they do.

Making any of these engine sounds will slow you down a bit and they all affect the way that your bike works, so they are just for fun – for larking around in the park or in your own street if it's safe and traffic-free. If you're going out on the open road, then dismantle your engine sound.

But if you are meeting up with your mates in the park or some other traffic-free zone, then text them beforehand and tell them to listen out for you arriving on your dirt bike!

Fantastic Fact or Fab Fib?

The fastest man on a bicycle has pedalled himself up to a speed of more than 269 kph (167 mph).

How to Get Out of Kissing Your Auntie

There's a fat old auntie or a great-aunt, a godmother or a crumbly old sister-in-law of your granny's cousin, in every family – and her visits give every kid nightmares. As soon as you're told she's coming, it's like a dark cloud blots out the sun, there's a clap of thunder and somebody starts playing weird organ music. The dog trembles, whimpers and turns grey, people in photographs look away and that toy bear you've had all your life puts on its duffle coat and catches the train back to darkest Peru.

It's not that she's entirely evil, although she could worship a seven-headed spider god and sacrifice kittens on an altar in her basement for all you know; and it's not that there's never an up-side to her visit – maybe some sort of gift or a tenner pressed into your hand. It's just THE KISS. She likes nothing better than

to give you a great big smacker right on the lips, or as near to the middle of your face as she can get it because she struggles to see past that great, blobby, powdered nose.

Fantastic Fact or Fab Fib?

The muscle you use to pucker your lips for a kiss is called the orbicularis oris.

It's the kiss that you can taste and smell for up to a week afterwards. It tastes of waxy lipstick and denture cleaner and smells like flowery violet perfume mixed with a whiff of stale milk from her last cup of tea. Worse than that, though, is how it feels. It's greasy and dry at the same time, wrinkly but firm, and if you're brave enough to keep your eyes open you can see the lips coming towards you, puckering up. Running from the top lip to the nose are crevasse-like lines overloaded with crumbly make-up and glistening with little stubbly hairs that prick into your face like you're being squashed against a wire brush.

And you can't get away. Try to turn your face and one of those podgy hands will have you by the chin faster than you can say Jabba the Hutt. Amazing how quickly those hands can move, isn't it? And, once you're trapped in the bear-hug, captured and smothering in the warm, moist embrace of the bingo wings, all you can do is hope that it's over with as quickly as possible.

On the other hand, you could make sure that she never wants to kiss you in the first place. The only way to do that is to make yourself utterly unkissable, and that means you're going to have to look pretty repulsive – even more repulsive than she is.

The thing to remember about old ladies is that they don't want to catch anything. Of course, no one in their right mind *wants* to get ill, but old ladies are especially frightened of it. Even though the thing that they like doing most is complaining about all their aches and pains and letting everyone know how much they suffer, they really don't want to catch even the slightest cold or a bit of a cough. They certainly don't want the kind of highly infectious-looking warty sores around the mouth that you are going to have. For the old dear, the sight of crusty sores on your face will really make her want to keep her distance. So, how do you suddenly develop hideously huge sores without contracting some equally hideous, horrible disease? It's easy – you fake them.

What you will need are a few Sugar Puffs, a glue stick of the white, slimy glue that you've probably used at school, some flesh-coloured make-up and a small make-up brush. If you don't like the sound of make-up, then face paints can always be used instead and, because of the range of colours, they can work even better.

Fantastic Fact or Fab Fib?

When people kiss there is an involuntary reflex action that makes their toes curl.

What you are going to do is use the Sugar Puffs to make warty, mole-like sores on your face. You can't use a whole Sugar Puff to make a sore because if you stick a few of them on your face it will just look as if you fell asleep in your breakfast. Whole Sugar Puffs are just too big; they stick out from your face and don't look at all convincing. All you really need is the tip of a Sugar Puff – the very end. Very carefully cut off the end using a sharp knife or a craft knife and you'll find you have a straight back to your Sugar Puff tip that allows it to be stuck flat on your face, but with a lovely, lined, gnarly outer surface – a perfect texture.

The texture might be good, but the colour isn't quite right. Sugar Puffs have light and dark areas where they have been toasted, which is good, but that's probably not going to blend with your skin very well. A convincing sore will have a pinkish, fleshy colour, so before you cut the tip off your Sugar Puff, paint it with a touch of fleshy-looking make-up or face paint. (Tip: It's easier to hold the Sugar Puff to paint it before you cut off the tip.) The light and dark areas should show through the new colour to give a natural effect, providing you don't slap on too much.

You need to use the same fleshy colour on your face just above or below your lip to create the site for your sore. Again, don't use too much colour. You only need a tiny amount to create a spot that looks inflamed. Gently rub around the edges of the spot to blend the colour into your skin. Then dab a little of the glue stick on the back of your Sugar Puff tip and stick it in the middle of your spot.

Only ever use the kind of white glue stick that you know from the classroom, which is non-toxic and will wash off. This is the only type of glue you should use.

NEVER USE SUPER GLUE!!!

In fact, never use any type of glue other than the non-toxic, water-soluble (that means it will dissolve in water to wash off) white glue sticks. If you have sensitive skin of any kind, then try testing a tiny amount of the glue and the make-up or face paints

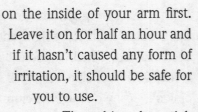

on the inside of your arm first. Leave it on for half an hour and if it hasn't caused any form of irritation, it should be safe for you to use.

The white glue stick will not keep your warty sores in place forever, but it will do the job for long enough for you to escape the clutches of your auntie. Once you have two or three in place around your mouth, check them out in a mirror. If you have some honey – the same stuff that you will use for a hay fever dodge in 'How to Get Out of Gardening' (page 59) – use the end of your brush to dab the tiniest blob of honey to the tip of your sore. It will glisten there like a lovely little glob of pus.

Naturally, you will have to practise in order to make your sores look real and you needn't only put them around your mouth. A couple on the side of your face will put your auntie off going for a peck on the cheek instead of a smacker on the lips.

Fantastic Fact or Fab Fib?

A teenage couple in Frankfurt, Germany, kissed while eating toffee apples at a fair, with the result that their lips stuck together. After a few minutes, the girl fainted and the lip-lock was broken. When asked what he did when his girlfriend was taken to the first aid station, the boy replied, 'I had a hot dog.'

How to Get Out
of Eating Sprouts

There are lots of things that you can look forward to when Christmas comes around, but eating sprouts with your festive dinner isn't one of them. You can look forward to getting your presents out from under the tree, ripping them open and acting surprised when you see what's in there. (Obviously you will already have squeezed, poked, rattled and peeked enough to have worked out what they all are.) You can look forward to all the sweets and treats on offer for weeks around this time of year – Christmas, after all, really kicks off around the beginning of November with Bonfire Night. You can even look forward to *giving* people presents because that usually means you'll get one in return. But no one looks forward to eating sprouts.

Sprouts are the worst of all vegetables. They are leafy, like

15

cabbage, but can have bits in them as hard as a raw carrot; they can be tough enough to need as much chewing as munching on an old wellie, but they can also be as slimy as the slugs that once crawled all over them; and they smell about as tasty as your PE teacher's socks. Why on earth would anyone want to eat them? 'They're GOOD for you!' is what the grown-ups say, but you have to suspect that they are only forcing you to eat sprouts because, when they were your age, someone forced them to do it, too.

Fantastic Fact or Fab Fib?

Brussels sprouts are traditionally grown in Belgium, taking their name from the capital of the country, but were almost certainly first cultivated in ancient Rome.

Strangely, some people do actually *enjoy* eating sprouts, but if the thought of having to swallow one makes your stomach start to spin faster than a runaway washing machine, you need to get out of eating sprouts. But you're going to have to be very brave.

One of the many, many problems with sprouts is that they are not easy to hide. They are too big to crush under your plate like peas and there's nowhere you can camouflage them amid leftover gravy, as you can with cabbage once you've chopped it up small enough. Secretly chopping cabbage underneath other food you are cutting is easy, but sprouts refuse to be covered up for sneaky slicing. You must also remember that the grown-ups will be watching to make sure you eat the sprouts. At Christmas time they turn into the Vegetable Police.

So, the best way to get out of eating sprouts is to make it look as if you actually really have eaten them. Start by making sure that you don't get a whole heap of them on your plate. 'Not too many sprouts for me, thank you' is a good thing to say. It's polite, but it's not a refusal, so it does look as if you're giving it a go. If you're lucky, you'll only get three or four. Now you need to get rid of them.

If you have a dog, you will already know that your four-legged friend is more than willing to help you out when it comes to disposing of unwanted food. But don't give sprouts to the dog. Within minutes, a large Labrador-type dog will let out a blast like a clap of thunder and fill the room with a stench that will make your eyes water. Just the thought of it makes me want to open a window. A smaller Yorkie-type dog may well send itself rocketing across the room with a very surprised look on its poor little face. Either way, all eyes will turn to you and the question will be asked: 'Who gave sprouts to the dog?' Sprouts make dogs fart – it's a well-known fact – but that's not always a bad thing. It can get you out of being blamed for a fart at Christmas dinner, for example. In any case, it is difficult to slip sprouts to the dog when the Vegetable Police have you under observation – it's even harder if you don't have a dog.

Fantastic Fact or Fab Fib?

Vegetables have long been thought to be good for you, but recent research has shown that peas can make you deaf and carrots may make your toenails drop out.

Unfortunately, the only way to do a convincing job of pretending to eat your sprouts is to actually put them in your mouth! Don't worry – they won't be there for long. What you have to do is plan ahead: you need to prepare for sprout disposal.

On Christmas Eve, begin laying your plans. Start sniffing as though you have a runny nose and talking as if you're a bit blocked up. You'll need to practise that in the same way that you have to practise your hay fever sneezing (see 'How to Get Out of Gardening', page 59). A couple of good sneezes on

Christmas Eve should be enough to let everyone know that you have a bit of a cold. Don't overdo it: your cold needs to come on slowly and not get too serious if you don't want to be grounded 'until you get over that chill' for the rest of the holidays.

Then, on Christmas morning and throughout the day, you will have to do a little more sneezing and nose-blowing. That sets the scene for Christmas dinner, when you must show true grit, spear one of those sprouts with your fork and then ... yes ... pop it in your mouth. Make a show of giving it a chew, moving it around your mouth a bit, then wrinkle your nose as though you are about to sneeze. Quickly reach into your pocket, pull out a hankie and cover your nose and mouth. When you sneeze, blow the sprout out into your hankie before stuffing the hankie in your pocket.

A word of caution about the sneeze: you mustn't make the sneeze too violent and you must have a strong hankie. A cloth hankie is strong, but you are likely to have only one in your pocket and it is difficult to use when it becomes overloaded with sprouts. Hardly anyone nowadays uses cloth hankies anyway, because paper ones are more hygienic – you dispose of them after one sneeze and don't carry bugs (or sprouts, in your case) around with you. Your paper hankie must, however, be good and strong. You don't want your sprout to tear straight through it, shoot across the table and plop into your dad's gravy, or down the top of Auntie's favourite dress.

Don't sneeze your sprouts one after the other. Pace yourself, use a fresh hankie each time, and after a bit of snuffling, say in a

bunged-up voice, 'Skuze me, I just neeb to blow by dose.' Then you trot off to the bathroom and flush the sprouts down the loo.

You just have to hope that, when you come back to the table, another three or four of the little green devils aren't sitting on your plate, having been served up in your absence by the Vegetable Police.

Fantastic Fact or Fab Fib?

In Ireland it is illegal to grow potatoes for boiling without a licence from the international boiled potato society, the Fédération Internationale de Boiling.

How to Win
at Noughts and
Crosses

Noughts and crosses is a game almost everyone knows how to play. It's a bit of a time-waster for when you have a few minutes to kill, and our ancestors have been playing it for more than 2,000 years – that's a lot of dead minutes!

Everyone will tell you that games are for fun and that it's the taking part that's important, not winning. WRONG! Naughty Kids don't take part in *any* game just for fun. Losing isn't fun, is it? Winning is fun. Crushing the opposition and seeing their faces fall when they realise that they have been utterly defeated – that's what a Naughty Kid calls fun. So, if you are going to take part in any game, you want to be in it to win it, and the best way to guarantee that you win, of course, is to CHEAT! Now we're talking proper fun ...

Before you can think about breaking the rules or any other kind of skulduggery, you first have to understand what you need to do to win. Noughts and crosses is a game of simple strategy and, if your opponent (the enemy) has even half a brain, he or she will very quickly realise what you have to do to avoid losing. Once the enemy is as clued up as that, under normal playing circumstances the best that you can hope for is a draw. If the enemy can maintain concentration, which shouldn't be a problem under normal playing circumstances, then he or she is unlikely to make a mistake. Clearly, we need to work out how to get rid of those pesky 'normal playing circumstances'.

Fantastic Fact or Fab Fib?

Archaeologists excavating in Rome have un-covered long-lost noughts and crosses grids chalked or scratched on ancient stonework.

First, however, you need to be an expert in the game. Unless you have been living on the planet Knickerbrain in the galaxy of Dingbatian all your life (in which case, welcome to our world, we hope you come in peace, and don't believe anyone who tells you that all Earthlings love sprouts), you are bound to have played or at least seen noughts and crosses being played. The rules, even for a Knickerbrain alien, are actually quite simple.

You draw a grid with two horizontal lines and two vertical lines, creating nine boxes – the grid is left open at the top, bottom and sides. Next, you decide who is to go first. The player who starts is 'X'. You could try to decide who is going to be 'X' by using Rock, Paper, Scissors (See 'How to Win at Rock, Paper, Scissors', page 109), but anyone who has played a Naughty Kid at that will probably never want to play them at anything else ever again. It might be best just to toss a coin. Try saying, 'Heads I win, tails you lose.' You never know, it might work on a Knickerbrain and that would be your first cheat!

If the enemy gives you the choice of going first, take it. The player who starts is always at an advantage because you will be first to play your third 'X' and first to play the crucial fourth 'X'. The object of the game is to take turns at putting an 'X' or, for the enemy, an 'O' in the boxes on the grid with the aim of being first to get three in a row horizontally, vertically or diagonally.

If you are starting as 'X', go for a corner. Any corner will do. NEVER start by putting your 'X' in the middle, which reduces your options and hands the advantage over to the enemy. Once you have grabbed a corner, if the enemy has any sense, he or she will put the first 'O' in the middle, as this reduces your options on the next move and prevents you from using the diagonals.

Fantastic Fact or Fab Fib?

If you were an officer and a gentleman serving with the Duke of Wellington's army during the Napoleonic Wars, you were banned from settling disputes by challenging your opponent to a duel. Two young officers who fell out decided to settle their grievances by playing noughts and crosses (best of five) but the loser was so angry that he leapt up, drew his sword and killed the winner. He was hanged for murder and an unfinished noughts and crosses game was carved on his tombstone.

Your second 'X' should go in another corner – not the one diagonally opposite your first 'X', as there's an 'O' between them now, but one that leaves you with two 'X's separated by a blank space. This keeps you in charge of the game. The enemy must now put an ' O ' between your two 'X's to block you. With the first 'O' having been placed in the middle, the enemy inevitably has two in a row and must be blocked with your next 'X'. You will then end up blocking each other and the game should finish as a draw, unless one of you isn't paying attention – perhaps a little distracted – and misses an obvious block.

If, however, you are starting as 'X' and you grab a corner but the enemy does not take the middle, you should win. All you have to do is plant your second 'X' in another corner that leaves a blank space between it and your first 'X'. The enemy must fill that blank to block you. Now grab a third corner and you are guaranteed to have two options for placing the vital fourth 'X'. The enemy will only be able to block one of them and you will win. Grabbing the corners is the key.

Having won, you should probably let the enemy have a go at being 'X' – but resist this at all costs. You can try saying, 'Winner always starts', or 'I'm X and X always starts'. This is a good CHEAT if you can get away with it. It is unlikely that any enemy is going to let that happen, though. The enemy will want to have a go at starting. When this happens, remember that, wherever the enemy puts the first 'X', you must grab the middle box. You then block all of the enemy's other moves. The best you can hope for if you are starting second is to draw, unless your enemy makes a big mistake, possibly because there has been some distraction.

Distractions? How can any kind of distraction really make a difference? I hear you ask. Distractions will make a difference because you will be causing them. This is the best CHEAT that you can pull. You need to put the enemy under pressure and distract them to spoil their concentration. That way they can miss a block and you can pounce to win the game.

The pressure part is easy. Noughts and crosses is a game that is supposed to be played quickly. You can't let the enemy spend ages pondering over their next move. Apart from anything else, that would be really, really, really, reeeeeeeeeeally BORING! Even in chess, a game that moves more slowly than the last maths lesson on a Friday afternoon, the players must make a move within a certain time limit. They have timers like alarm clocks to keep them on their toes, and you need something similar, except that it needs to be something that the enemy will find really loud, and unbearably annoying. Nothing is louder or more annoying than a Naughty Kid, so you will turn yourself into a human timer. In any case, you're unlikely to have a clock or watch to hand that you can both see at the same time, so volunteer your services as a timer.

You need to agree that you have three seconds to make a move. That is more than enough time to decide where you are putting an 'X' or an 'O'. The easiest way to count seconds is by using a word that takes about a second to say. You could say, 'One crocodile, two crocodile, three crocodile', and that would take about three seconds. That's not very distracting, though, is it? You need to spoil the enemy's concentration and to do that you have to be loud. Shouting 'ONE CROCODILE!' might work, but it's better to find something that will totally upset the enemy. If the enemy has pets, try 'ONE DEAD KITTEN! TWO DEAD KITTENS! THREE DEAD KITTENS!' That will work with puppies, too, or canaries, or squashed snakes. If the enemy is not the type to get upset about dead pets, then you need to attack some other weakness. He or she could be hungry, in which case 'ONE SAUSAGES! TWO PANCAKES! THREE PIZZA!' might do the trick. If he or she is desperate to go to the loo, then a simple shusssssshing sound could be your best option.

What you are trying to do is force the enemy to make a mistake so that you can win. Distracting the enemy or putting them off their game is a despicable way of cheating, but thoroughly effective and highly recommended. The enemy may well become very angry and start shouting about not wanting to play with you any more. At this point, all you need to say is, 'So, you concede?' Conceding is the same as surrendering. If the enemy surrenders, then you have won. Well done!

Fantastic Fact or Fab Fib?

The maximum number of 'X's (or 'O's) that you can fit on a noughts and crosses board without having three in a row is six.

How to Watch
Telly Past
Your Bedtime

You know it's coming. You're sitting there watching telly with your mum and dad and then, halfway through a movie or just as one of your favourite shows is about to start, you hear the dreaded 'It's a school night'. You're sent off to bed with no excuses and no arguments. Harsh! They will sit up and watch TV for hours to come, but you have no option but to do as you're told and you're not allowed to watch TV in your room, even if you are lucky enough to have one there. It's almost cruel.

Arguing will only cause a row and then you won't get to watch what you wanted to anyway. So don't argue – just leave the room. You have to object a bit, otherwise it would look suspicious. It would look as if you were giving in too easily. So put up a bit of resistance, leave the room and then put your plan into action to get back in the room where the TV is. This isn't going to be easy, mainly because your parents are still in there, but you can do it if you plan ahead and prepare properly.

The first thing that you have to do – way before the day when you know you will want to stay up late – is find somewhere to hide in the living room. Behind a sofa, behind the curtains or in a cupboard are possible options, but it must be somewhere that will be out of sight of your parents when they are sitting watching telly. It also has to be somewhere with a view of the telly, otherwise it's no good at all!

Fantastic Fact or Fab Fib?

Television was invented by Simon Cowell in 1876.

Once you've chosen your secret spot, it may be that you need a bit of help to see the TV without sticking your head out from behind the sofa and immediately being spotted by your parents. This is where a periscope could come in handy, and they're pretty easy to make.

What you need is a long, thin cardboard box. The box that a roll of kitchen foil comes in is ideal. These boxes open all down one side for dispensing the foil, so once it is empty, you have to tape the opening closed. This taped side and the opposite side of the box will form the left and right sides of your periscope; the other two sides will be the front and back.

Next, use scissors or a craft knife to cut a 'window' at the top end of the front of the periscope. Make this window as wide as you can without taking it right out to the very edges of the box. It should be about a centimetre from the top of the box and about a centimetre deep. Now you need to slice off the 'lid' of your periscope, but at an angle. Start at the very top, above your window, and cut along the fold that joins the two front corners. Then, from each of these corners, cut down towards the back of the periscope at an angle of forty-five degrees (if you then cut straight across the back, you should be able to remove the end of the box so that the top of your periscope is now slanting from front to back at a forty-five-degree angle). Now tape a small mirror or mirror card across the hole at the top, forming a sloping 'roof' for the periscope, with the mirrored surface facing the inside.

At the bottom of the periscope, make another small window, this time in the back. You then cut off the bottom, again at an angle of forty-five degrees, from the bottom edge below your back window up to the front, so you will be creating a long, thin parallelogram. Tape another mirror to the bottom to form a base. The idea is that light comes in through the top window and is reflected off the top mirror down inside the box until it hits the bottom mirror and bounces out through the bottom window. If you look through the bottom window, you should be able to see whatever the top window is pointing at.

Using your periscope, you will be able to peek out from behind the curtains or the sofa, or even see out from behind a cupboard door if it is left slightly open – just wide enough for you to poke the top of your periscope out.

Your periscope needs to be left in position in your hiding place in advance, where you can get your hands on it quickly as soon as you conceal yourself there.

So you've found a suitable hiding place and put your periscope there, should you need to use it, but having been sent off to bed, how do you get back into the room again without being spotted? Clearly, you need to be able to get your parents out of the way long enough for you to sneak back in. What you need is some kind of distraction that will make them both leave the room, and here are a couple of ideas about how you might do that.

If you live in a house where you have an upstairs and you are sent upstairs to bed, you might be able to lure your parents to the back door of the house. You need to make a loud, strange and annoying noise outside the back door to force them to get up and investigate. You can make just such a noise using a biscuit tin and a couple of spoons. Put the spoons inside the biscuit tin and tape the lid shut. They will rattle about in there and make a great noise. Now you need a long piece of strong string. Tie it around the biscuit tin as though you are tying up a parcel (you can also tape the string in place to make it totally secure). You need a really long piece of string to lower the biscuit tin out of an upstairs window, preferably a window that is right above the back door.

Lower the tin quietly and then jiggle it about a bit to make the spoons clatter around inside the tin. This should make enough noise for one of your parents to come and take a look outside. You have to pull the tin back up before they get to the back door. Obviously, they mustn't see the tin. The first time you jangle your biscuit tin outside the back door, your mum or dad will probably take a look, shrug and go back inside. Give them a couple of minutes to get settled down, then lower

your biscuit tin and jangle it again. This time they will be a bit more concerned by the noise, but will probably take only a brief look outside. Let them get back to the living room again before giving them another jangle. By this time, they will be really annoyed and will be outside, maybe with torches, having a good look around to see what's making the noise.

While they are doing that, you have to move fast, get downstairs and into your hiding place before they come back in again. If you stay as quiet as a mouse, you should be safe enough until they go off to bed, at which point you can sneak back to your own bed again.

If you live in a flat or the biscuit tin outside the back door isn't going to work, then try getting your parents out of the way by sending them out the front door. You can do that by making the doorbell ring. You don't need to interfere with the bell mechanism at all – that's almost certainly something that your parents would spot when they go to answer the door for the second or third time. What you can do is to record the sound of the doorbell on your phone or some other device, hold it outside your bedroom door and press 'play'. If you can get it loud enough, the fake doorbell should get your parents away from the telly for long enough for you to dart in quickly.

You have to move fast and quietly when you're racing to your hiding place – and then, for goodness' sake, don't fall asleep and start snoring or you'll be well and truly busted!

Fantastic Fact or Fab Fib?

Electrical impulses in your brain can be used to boost the signal from your TV remote when the batteries are running low, simply by holding the back of the remote against your forehead when you push the buttons.

How to Get
Out of Listening to
Your Parents' Music
in the Car

There isn't a single thing that you and your brothers or sisters can do to annoy your parents on a long car journey. Nope, not one single thing – there are HUNDREDS! Some of the things that they get annoyed about are totally unfair. Sitting in the back of the car is the ideal time for you to get out your phone, music player or games gizmo, plug in your earphones and drive your own car, crush some candy, deal with the flappy bird, slaughter some zombies or work on some puzzles – all of which are actually good brain training.

Do your parents want you to do that? Of course they don't.

They might even have invested in DVD screens for the back of the car so that you can plug your earphones into that and watch a movie or enjoy some cartoons.

Do your parents want you to do that? Of course they don't.

So what do they want you to do? Have a snooze? Definitely not! Eat crisps and chocolate? Not a chance. Read a book? Even that's been knocked on the head.

> Fantastic Fact or Fab Fib?
> Cars have metal strips moulded into the rubber of their tyres in order to make digital radio reception possible.

You might hear the famous words, 'Why don't you look out the window? You might learn something.' Well, that's not what they tell you at school, is it? If you sit and stare out the window in class you're likely to have the teacher barking in your ear and a half-hour detention after school. Staring out the window is not a good habit to get into. In any case, what your parents probably most want is to have a nice chat about what you can see from the car as you drive along, although there's not much to say about mile after mile of motorway crash barrier. They might want to chat about what you're going to do when you get to wherever you're going, although that can probably be covered in five minutes while they're sorting out coats, keys, wallets, handbags and suchlike in the car park. They might even want to talk about what you've been up to at school – and that's definitely to be avoided.

Their ultimate goal is to tune the car radio to a station so boring that only old people know how to find it. Then they'll try to get you to sing along to songs so ancient that Noah's family were probably humming them while they counted the animals onto the ark.

You have to put a stop to this 'family sing-song' nonsense as quickly as possible and the way to do it is to sing a song of your own. If you have brothers or sisters who can join you in this, then it works even better.

Fantastic Fact or Fab Fib?

In the state of Illinois, in America, it is illegal to join in a song on the radio when driving. You can be fined for having a singalong as it is regarded as a dangerous distraction, but there is no law against reading a newspaper while driving.

Everybody knows the old family favourite, 'The Wheels on the Bus'. Everybody knows it, but you'll struggle to find anyone who admits to liking it. Don't worry, you're not going to have to sing it, but you do need to remember the music. Fix that little tune in your head – remember how it goes?

The wheels on the bus go round and round
Round and round

Rod Green

Round and round
The wheels on the bus go round and round
All day long

Got it? Good – now you can forget those words and substitute
the following, to the same tune:

We know a song that'll get on your nerves
Get on your nerves
Get on your nerves
We know a song that'll get on your nerves
All day long

But you don't stop there. You have to keep it going, loud and
without a pause ...

We know a song that'll get on your nerves
Get on your nerves
Get on your nerves
We know a song that'll get on your nerves
All day long

We know a song that'll get on your nerves
Get on your nerves
Get on your nerves
We know a song that'll get on your nerves
All day long

We know a song that'll get on your nerves
Get on your nerves
Get on your nerves
We know a song that'll get on your nerves
All day long

We know a song that'll get on your nerves
Get on your nerves
Get on your nerves
We know a song that'll get
on your nerves
All day long

There is no other part to the song. This is all you sing, over and over and over again. It will, of course, get on their nerves quite a bit and by the time you've run through ten or twelve repeats, they will be begging you to shut up, plug in your earphones and do whatever you were going to do in the first place.

However annoying they might have thought you were when you were minding your own business, they will now feel the relief of having a quiet rear seat and leave you in peace.

Fantastic Fact or Fab Fib?

In 1979, singer Gary Numan released a single called 'Cars', the lyrics of which were written after he experienced a road rage incident.

How to Get
Out of Sitting in
the Middle

The smallest one has to sit in the middle. That's the rule when the whole family piles into the car for an outing, whether you're simply off shopping or setting out on a holiday car journey that could take hours. This is pretty tough on you if you are the smallest one. It's even worse if you're not the smallest one and the rules are suddenly changed so that you have to suffer on the seat-that's-not-really-a-real-seat between your brothers and sisters. Why should you have to do that if you're not the smallest? Because the smallest one has suddenly come over a bit weak, wibbly and sickly and needs to be beside a window, or has simply gone into meltdown with a massive tantrum. That's when your parents start using phrases like 'Just this once', 'It's only fair' and 'Please, just for me'.

At this stage, if you're the smallest, well done – mission accomplished! If, on the other hand, you're the smallest, you've tried every trick you know and you're *still* heading for the middle, read on. Or, if you're not the smallest but you think there's a chance you might be banished to the middle seat anyway, this is how you get out of it.

Fantastic Fact or Fab Fib?

Your nose is far more sensitive than you think and sitting too close to people for too long irritates scent receptors in the nose, which send a message to the brain that makes you hate the person next to you.

What you're going to do is bumble towards the car with a droopy-eyed, slack-faced expression, complaining that you're not feeling too good. Then, you're going to make a huge barfing noise and puke up in a flowerbed, on the grass, in the gutter or anywhere in the vicinity of the car. No one in their right mind is going to force a kid who's just produced a fairly impressive pavement pizza to sit in the middle – the risk of another eruption is just too great. In an emergency, a sick child can puke out the window. The last thing any parent wants is the kid in the middle being sick: they can't reach a window and puking into a bag is just messy. The real nightmare is the kid who tries to hold it in, clamps a hand across his or her mouth and produces a five-finger fountain that hoses the entire inside of the car. Yes, provided that you assure everyone that you are feeling strong enough to travel, throwing up outside the car pretty much guarantees you a window seat.

So how do you puke right on cue? You simply can't make yourself sick to order, can you? No, you can't. You may have heard of all sorts of things that you can eat to make yourself vomit. Ignore them.

NEVER EAT ANYTHING THAT WILL MAKE YOU ILL.

Your objective here is to get yourself a window seat, not an ambulance bed.

What you are going to do is to *fake* a vomit.

Fantastic Fact or Fab Fib?

The first car manufacturer to fit modern seat belts to a car as standard equipment was the Swedish company Volvo in 1959.

You will need a small tin of vegetable soup. You don't want the creamy stuff, what you need is straightforward vegetable soup that has an overall reddish brown colour and plenty of diced carrots, which, as every fool knows, always seem to turn up in a pile of vomit for some reason. You will also need a long, straight balloon. A party balloon is fine. It doesn't matter what colour as no one is going to see it. Cut the open end off the balloon – the bit you would use to blow it up – then use a funnel to fill the balloon with cold soup. You shouldn't need too much, just a reasonable puke's worth. Don't overfill the balloon, you need to leave enough empty balloon at the top to be able to hold it shut so that the soup doesn't come out until you want it to.

A balloon full of soup is wobbly and difficult to handle, but it can be carried more easily and kept more stable if you put it inside a sock. Then what you have to do is to hide your soup-filled sock balloon up your sleeve. You need to try to keep it upright to avoid spillage, so if you have it up your right sleeve, hold your right hand to the side of your face. It will help you to look poorly. Use your left hand as though gripping your right wrist but secretly pinch the top of the balloon closed to keep the soup inside.

Then, before you get too close to your waiting family, deliver your 'I'm really not feeling very well' line, turn away from them, bend over and make a huge retching noise. This is a barf that has to sound like it has come from deep inside you, not just from your mouth, your throat, your chest or even your stomach. Deeper. Somewhere down around your knees, maybe. Practise when no one is listening.

Record it and play it back to make sure that you are getting the right sort of booming tone.

Just as you deliver the barf, having turned away so that no one can see where it's coming from, point your sleeve at the ground, let the end of the balloon poke out and squeeze the sock. The soup will hit the deck with the same sort of force as a real chunder. Tuck the balloon away safely up your sleeve and turn to everyone and say bravely, 'Well, maybe that was all it needed. I think I'll be okay now.'

You might be okay, but no one in his/her right mind is going to want you sitting in the middle!

Fantastic Fact or Fab Fib?

In major cities like New York, London and Paris there are huge rat populations with at least two rats for every person, although the rats are seldom seen. On the roads, at least one car in three will have a rat living in the seat upholstery.

How to Get Your Dog to Actually Eat Your Homework

*Y*ou *meant* to do it, didn't you? You had every intention of sitting down and concentrating on it so you could get through it all in one big effort, but other things just kept getting in the way – things that were a lot more interesting. Well, pretty much anything is more interesting than doing homework, isn't it? Watching your fingernails grow is more interesting than homework.

The trouble is that teachers have made it much more difficult to dodge doing your homework nowadays. The old excuse of 'I forgot to bring it' doesn't really work when you were set homework that had to be done on your PC and emailed to the teacher. Even if you are working on something that might be too big to email you will be expected to bring it to school on some kind of flash drive and if the homework involved working on one of the websites that the school uses, they can check that you did it without you having to bring anything to school. Sometimes they even set online homework where the teacher can actually watch while you're doing it! What's the world coming to? The classroom just invaded your bedroom! Is nowhere safe?

Naturally, a true Naughty Kid will be able to find ways round the modern-day homework problem. You can't email homework to the teacher or do anything online if you can't actually get online, so having 'a problem with our broadband at home' can work temporarily. Forgetting or losing passwords to access websites, forgetting to attach an email attachment or 'accidentally' hitting Delete instead of Send are mistakes that people really do make every day, but, like any homework excuse, a catalogue of blunders and lapses of memory will only buy you a little more time. If you say you've done the work but can't produce it, you will simply be asked to hand it in the following day. To get round any technical problems you may claim to be having at home, your teacher might even set you homework that needs to be done the old-fashioned way – written out by hand on sheets of paper.

'*Nooooooo!*' I hear you scream. 'Not the dreaded pen and paper!' Relax, it's a good thing. Any teacher who forces you to write out your homework with ink and paper is actually playing right into your hands. Some teachers, of course, will always set homework this way, and if you use all of the excuses above relating to computer failures, you can drag even the most tech-loving twenty-first-century educators back into the last millennium.

Homework that has been written out by hand can easily be ruined and made totally illegible if it is 'accidentally' dropped in a puddle on the way to school. It's a pretty lame excuse because, for the ink to run and the paper to get really soggy, your homework would have to be swimming around in that puddle for quite some time, wouldn't it? The teacher will want to know why you didn't rescue it before it became a total mess. Well, it blew all over the pavement, didn't it? That's how it got so muddy, and every time you bent down to pick it up, it blew further away again. Of course, this dodge depends heavily on the weather. If it hasn't rained, there won't be any puddles. In any case, the teacher is quite likely to say, 'Well, if you did such a good job – two whole sides of A4 – then it will all be fresh in your mind. You can stay behind after school and it won't take you long to write it out again.'

You will get the same result if you try handing in a washed-out, horribly stained homework sheet and say that the cat 'knocked a glass of orange juice all over it while I was out of the room'. Obviously, you not being present would give the orange juice, or Coke, or Ribena (a truly stain-worthy drink) time to do the utmost damage and obliterate anything on the page. Unfortunately, any kind of soggy offering or dried-out, shrivelled-up 'accident' is going to get the same reaction as the puddle pages – and, frankly, that's no more than these poor excuses deserve.

Teachers, you see, are not fools (well, not *all* of them!) and it is rumoured that many of them were once youngsters themselves. Once upon a time, some of them may even have been Naughty Kids! They will certainly have tried to dodge doing their own homework, back in the Dark Ages. Over the years these teachers have seen pupils come and go, trying all sorts of dodges to cover up the fact that they haven't done their homework. They know all the tricks; they see kids wriggling and squirming and telling whopping great lies the whole time. If you try any of the scams above, they will look at you like you are making a truly pathetic attempt to pull the wool over their eyes and mark you down for detention faster than the speed of light.

Fantastic Fact or Fab Fib?

As far as scientists have been able to discover, nothing travels faster than the speed of light. Light travels at more than 299,338 kilometres (186,000 miles) per second. To give you some idea of how fast that is, the circumference of the Earth is about 40,000 kilometres (25,000 miles) and light could, therefore, travel right around the world more than seven times in just one second.

What can we learn from this? Well, the 16th President of the United States, Abraham Lincoln, is sometimes quoted as having said, 'You can fool all of the people some of the time, and some of the people all of the time, but you cannot fool all the people all of the time.' If he ever did actually say that, then Lincoln was definitely a Naughty Kid when he was younger. What he said about 'people' also applies to teachers, most of whom count as people; the rest come from a strange planet in a galaxy far, far away. The point is, you will have to judge what your teacher is like and work out the best dodge to use for that particular teacher.

There is one scam, however, that even the most battle-hardened, sly and savvy teacher will love to see you use. Any teacher who grew up as a Naughty Kid is certainly not going to fall for it but if you do it well, it will be hugely appreciated. Merely having the nerve to go for it will earn you huge respect: what you are handing over is less a piece of homework than a work of art. What is this five-star, gold-plated king of excuses? It is, of course, 'The Dog Ate My Homework'.

This is not an easy dodge to pull off – especially if you don't have a dog – but it is well worth the effort. The first thing that you are going to need is a dog. If you don't have one, you will need to borrow one. Everyone knows someone who has a dog and if that someone isn't already a friend, you need to make friends. Clearly, this could take some advance planning because you need to get to the stage where you can offer to take the dog for a walk. That's a big responsibility and you might think it's a bit of a chore, but once you have made friends with a dog, it will be your friend forever and that's not such a bad thing. Anyway, befriending a dog is a small price to pay for pulling off this dodge!

Fantastic Fact or Fab Fib?

In an attempt to prove that raindrops are wetter than tap water, Italian Alessandro Reggazoni from Milan held one hand out of his apartment window and the other under a running tap in his kitchen. Reggazoni was struck by lightning but survived, only to fall out of the fourth-floor window. He landed on a canopy stretched out over a shop window at street level and bounced onto the pavement. After suffering only minor bruises and a scorched hand from the lightning strike, he is now known as 'Lucky' Reggazoni.

Once you have a dog on your side, you need to prepare your homework paper. You will have to write a few lines at the top of the sheet that will look like whatever homework you were expected to do. Use a ballpoint pen but test the pen first to make sure that the ink will 'run' when it is wet: mark a few scribbles on a sheet of paper and then soak it in water in the kitchen sink. On your finished, dog-eaten paper, you want to give the idea that the slobbering hound left the remnants of your homework so completely drenched with doggy drool that you can hardly read a word of it.

It may be that you have to compose a few lines of an essay or even work out a few sums of maths to make the surviving scraps of homework look real. Don't do too much 'real' stuff – you are supposed to be using this dodge to get out of doing your homework, after all! Once you have a few lines that look like you made a proper effort to do your homework, you can then write a load of nonsense on the next few lines because they will be obliterated by the dog slobber and pretty much torn to pieces as well.

Once you have prepared your fake homework, don't immediately soak it in water. First, you need to get a few bite marks on it and for that you need a dog. Don't try to bite the paper yourself because your bite marks will never look anything like those produced by a dog. So how do you persuade your dog (or your borrowed dog) to chew up the paper? Dogs, like teachers, are not completely stupid. They do like to chew things, but they generally go for things that smell and taste good – to them, at least. Bones, sticks and sweaty socks are some top tail-waggy favourites! You might think that paper is fairly low down the list of things dogs normally like to eat, but lots of dogs love to chew up paper, so getting the dog interested couldn't be simpler.

All you have to do is rub the paper with a dog treat, a little of the dog's food or even a small piece of burger or bacon that you sneaked off your plate at dinner time. Once the paper smells tasty, scrunch the bottom part slightly so that you can waft it about in front of him. The dog will, no doubt, think that this is a great game and start grabbing at the paper with his teeth. He will try to pull the paper away from you and you should let him, otherwise it will end up completely ripped to shreds. You need to try to keep the top part, where your fake homework is, as intact as possible.

Don't let the dog run off with the paper. You need to do all this in a room (your bedroom is probably best for secrecy) so the dog can't escape. If he gets away, he might really eat the paper before you can stop him, and that wouldn't be good for the poor dog or for your homework dodge (although most dogs prefer to shred paper rather than swallow it). Your job now is to get the paper back from him with a selection of good teeth marks in it, but before he can chew it up completely. You know best how to deal with your own dog, but offering him a dog treat or some food will almost certainly make him lose interest in the paper.

Now you have a homework sheet that is bitten and ripped, all you have to do is to tear off the bottom part of the sheet, where most of your homework would have been. This will be the part that the dog 'ate' and needs to look like it was snatched from his jaws, so you must tear it off in an uneven line, then scrunch up the rest and set to work carefully soaking the paper to make the ink run.

Fantastic Fact or Fab Fib?

The tallest dog ever was called Giant George, a Great Dane who was more than two metres (seven feet) tall when he stood on his hind legs and who became so famous that he appeared on *The Oprah Winfrey Show* on TV.

Lay the remains of your battle-scarred, ravaged, tattered homework sheet on an old towel to dry. With its bite marks, torn-off bottom and slobber-damaged ink, this is now an achievement of which you should be proud. When you present this to the teacher as 'evidence' that the dog ate your homework, it should look totally convincing and your teacher will be suitably sympathetic. The teacher might even excuse you from doing that particular piece of homework, if you are really lucky.

Sadly, those teachers who were once Naughty Kids themselves are unlikely to be fooled. The best that you can hope for from one of them is that they will be impressed with your workmanship and the effort you've put into creating your evidence. You may then gain their respect, although they are more likely to point out that it would have been far less effort simply to have done the homework in the first place!

But where's the fun in that?

How to Get Out of Gardening

If you are lucky enough to have a garden, then you'll know that gardens are for kicking a ball around or lazing in the sunshine and they're pretty cool places to hang out, right? Wrong! Gardens are torture chambers of endless chores that you will be forced into doing – picking up leaves, cutting the grass, watering plants or, the most tedious horror of all, WEEDING!

If you're caught with no place to hide and you know that you are about to be ordered outside to slave away with your hands in the mud among slithery worms and creatures with more running legs than the World Cup final, you need to think and act fast.

You're not going to get away with claiming to be injured or ill – not if you want to be allowed to watch TV later, go round to see your friends to play Grand Theft Auto and do whatever else you'd rather be doing – but there is one affliction that you can claim to have that will keep you out of the garden. It's something that makes even the toughest of parents think twice about forcing anyone to go outdoors ... hay fever.

Fantastic Fact or Fab Fib?

In 1973, champion gardener Mrs Eileen Wright from West Yorkshire in England grew a tulip six metres (twenty feet) high.

Never been known to suffer from hay fever? Your parents will know whether you are prone to getting hay fever, right? Wrong again! Hay fever is one of those things that can affect anyone at any time from early spring to late summer. Basically, it's a kind of allergy caused by pollen. Hay fever sufferers can be allergic to one particular kind of pollen, which means that they will only be affected for a very short period when the particular plant that causes their allergic reaction releases its pollen. They can have hay fever one day, but not the next. If they are allergic to more than one kind of pollen, they can then have another bout of hay fever a few days, or weeks, later. That makes hay fever a handy dodge that you can use time and time again – whenever gardening duties beckon – while apparently making a complete recovery in between.

So what are the most obvious symptoms of hay fever? Well, there are three – repeated mega-sneezes powerful enough to turn a wind turbine; watery, puffy eyes that look like you've been crying for a week; and enough snot streaming from your nose to make your mum want to take away your paper hankies and just give you a bucket! Fake these symptoms in a convincing way and you'll never have to work in the garden again.

Sneezing seems like the easiest to do, but needs a lot of practice for it to sound right. You have to suck in a huge lungful of air and bark it out again with a fair amount of noise. And you will have to decide what kind of noise best suits you, from the quieter 'Chooooooooo!' that sounds like a large wet sock flying past to the massive, double-bark 'Grraaa-Chuff!!' that sounds like a Great Dane fell out of the sky and landed on a Rottweiler.

Fantastic Fact or Fab Fib?

Henri Blanc, a grandfather from Marseilles in France, had never been in trouble with the law until he caught a cold in 1987. He was walking down the street when he sneezed so hard that his false teeth flew out and bit a policeman in the back of the neck. Henri was charged with assault and fined 50 euros.

The traditional way to fake watery eyes is to chop up an onion. Chopping onions makes nearly everyone cry but it seems hardly

likely that you'll have time to start chopping onions just before you get the call to go gardening. Neither is it something you can do in secret. Someone's going to notice if you show up crying your eyes out and stinking like the back of a burger van. There are lots of things that people might tell you will make your eyes go puffy, but don't listen to them.

NEVER PUT ANYTHING IN YOUR EYES!

For a convincingly puffy, watery look about the eyes, use a little eye make-up or face paint in a reddish-pinkish shade on your eyelids and just below your eyes. Don't go mad and end up looking like you've been on a night out with the cast of *The Vampire Diaries*, just make it seem a bit red around your eyes. Then carefully dab a very small smear of Vaseline underneath. This will make your eyes look moist, especially if you flick a few drops of water around them as well. Then, just screw up your eyes as though you are squinting in strong sunlight and they will look puffy.

Now for the snotty nose ... You will have to practise making it sound as if you are blowing your nose nice and loud. Cover your nose and mouth with a hankie and give a good rasp with your lips into cupped hands. Don't actually blow your nose because between your nose and your top lip you are going to have a very convincing, moist, glistening, slow-moving nostril slug. The best way to fake a snot creature emerging from your nose is to use honey. A blob of honey (you have to use the solid, natural honey, not the runny stuff – that won't stay in place) below one or both nostrils looks like the inside of your entire head has turned into a snot factory and is pumping the stuff out through your nostrils. Honey is easy to wipe off and looks truly disgusting – just what you want!

Honey does, of course, come in different colours and you don't want to use something that looks too yellow; a lighter colour is best. Highly colourful snot – the proper green stuff – actually shows you have some sort of infection and hay fever sufferers produce much clearer nose juice, so go easy on the colour.

When you're called to come and help with the gardening, be sure you can be heard sneezing as you make your way there. Then fake the nose blowing and, once you're convinced you've got everyone's attention, pull your hankie away to reveal your revolting snotty nose and screwed-up, puffy eyes. Who won't believe you when you say, 'I think I've got hay fever ...'?

Fantastic Fact or Fab Fib?

The Hanging Gardens of Babylon are famously known as one of the original Seven Wonders of the World, but no one knows exactly where they might have been. They may have been in the ancient city of Babylon (now Hillah in Iraq) or could possibly have been in Mosul, about four hundred and two kilometres (two hundred and fifty miles) north of Baghdad in Iraq.

How to Get Your Parents to Give You Double Pocket Money

For the most part, coaxing pocket money out of your parents' pockets into your own can be as tricky as pulling an elephant through a keyhole, but getting them to give you it *twice*? Impossible! Well, maybe not, but you have to pick your moment, and knowing the right one to pick is crucial. Apart from your preparation and planning, there are three stages to this dodge: the first hit, the second hit and the danger zone.

The first thing that you have to do is to take control of the pocket money situation. Most parents will wait until they are asked for the cash rather than simply hand it over and you must make sure that you always ask – in the nicest, politest way possible, of course. If you can make it so that your mum or dad gets used to the monetary exchange happening when you ask for it, then you can be in control of when the weekly transaction takes place.

Next, you have to use all your skills of observation. You need to strike when the parent who's in charge of pocket money is at their weakest. This may be when your mum comes home on a Friday night after a long week at work, or when Dad returns from a couple of drinks in the pub with his friends to celebrate the start of the weekend for example. Don't ask them for pocket money when they are happy and on top of the world – not if your ultimate aim is to hit them twice for the cash. A contented parent might bung you a little extra wonga, which is no bad thing, but to stay in control, you need to ask for the dosh when they're a bit weary. This is your first hit.

Fantastic Fact or Fab Fib?

The word 'dosh' is an acronym of 'dollars or silver handy'. If you say, 'I haven't got any dosh', you are actually saying, 'I haven't got any dollars or silver handy.'

Other weak points might be when they're a bit dozy after a big meal, after they've just watched a sad movie (especially if it features any kid who's having a hard time), or after they've seen the news with images of unfortunate refugees on the screen.

The point is to ask in the evening when they're not as bright and alert as they probably are around, say, lunchtime. Evenings are always best for the first hit.

You need to make the second hit first thing in the morning. When your dad's just got out of bed and his hair (if he still has any, with a kid like you plaguing him all the time!) looks like a cross between Sideshow Bob and a patch of nettles. You have to move in hard and fast. The second hit is a 'surgical strike' – quick, precise and executed without hesitation. To do that, you must be up early, way before your dad wakes. You also have to get your story straight. Plan what you are going to say and make it totally believable. You need to say you're off to meet your friends, Saturday morning cinema, shopping, swimming – anything that sounds plausible – but you're in a hurry and you're running late. Then you give him your double-money line: 'I don't think we sorted out my pocket money last night, did we, Dad? Could I have it now, please, because I really need to get going.'

This is a big fat lie and to get away with it you will have to practise what you intend to say. Do it in front of a mirror. Try to get that pleading, innocent look in your eyes and also practise looking anxious. Shift from one foot to the other as though you are desperate to get going, have your coat or bag in your hand and make sure that you time your attack so that you 'accidentally' bump into him in the hallway just as he's heading for the bathroom.

Fantastic Fact or Fab Fib?

The world's first flushing toilet was invented by an English engineer and plumber called Thomas Crapper.

Hopefully, you will have caught him in that early-morning, bleary state where he won't really be able to remember if he already gave you your pocket money or not, or even whether it's his job to do so. Did he hand over the cash last night, or is he thinking of last week? If you can pull it all off convincingly, he'll be so flustered that he will head back into the bedroom and grab some cash for you, happy to get you out of his face so that he can get to the bathroom.

Remember, timing is the key. Both of your hits have to happen when your mum or dad are at their most vulnerable – tired in the evening or groggy in the morning – and the second hit has to be a slick operation. The worst thing that can happen is that he or she will suddenly become very awake and say, 'Hang on a minute … I definitely gave you that last night because it was the last of my cash/change from the fish and chips/all in coins …' or some such highly accurate recollection. You are then well and truly rumbled and the only thing you can do is to turn on the charm, give him a big grin and say, 'Ha! Nearly had you there!'

Similarly, your mum or dad's moment of total recall may come once they've woken up later in the day and they will corner you about it then. This is deep in the danger zone. You don't want to look like you've hoodwinked them, so you have to make sure that you DO NOT SPEND the loot from the second hit. When you are in the danger zone, you have to have that cash ready to hand back, so that you can pull the same line as you would have done if you'd been busted in the morning: 'Almost fooled you there!' Having the cash ready at all times when you are in the danger zone makes it look as if you always had every intention of handing it back and this might just get you off the hook.

The danger zone is unlikely to last for more than a couple of days, but if you can hold onto the cash all week, until you are into the next round of pocket money, you're safe.

Of course, this is a thoroughly dishonest thing to do, but that's why this handbook is for despicable Naughty Kids and not delightful Do-Gooders.

Fantastic Fact or Fab Fib?

In 2002, the euro took over completely from a whole load of European currencies, making the mark, franc, lira, escudo and schilling no longer legal tender.

How to Make Somebody Do a Chicken Impression

*Y*ou can't make someone act like a chicken without them realising it ... or can you? The key to getting people to do what you want them to do is either to hold their goldfish to ransom, or to make them feel clever by convincing them that they are doing something that everyone says simply can't be done. Kidnapping the goldfish is fraught with danger – what if it turns out to be a piranha in disguise? Best stick to persuading them that they are smart.

Just ask any evil criminal mastermind (if you can find one that hasn't already been outwitted by Mr Holmes, Mr Bond or the Agents of S.H.I.E.L.D.): fooling people into doing what you want them to do means making them think that they are doing what THEY want, not what YOU want them to. They will definitely want to do something if they believe it will make people think they are clever. All of that means you are going to have to tell a few, very convincing, little lies.

Fantastic Fact or Fab Fib?

In Arizona, in America in the 1940s, a chicken called Mike lived for one and a half years after his head had been cut off.

So how do you make a lie convincing? Well, you have to practise. Try this:

1. Stand in front of the bathroom mirror.
2. Make a 'gun hand' and stick your forefinger gun barrel to your own forehead.
3. Now look yourself straight in the eyes and say, 'Nobody move or the kid gets it!'

Rubbish, isn't it? No matter how good an actor you are, you are never going to persuade yourself or anyone else that you can do yourself any damage with a finger pretending to be a gun, even if that finger is loaded. For a lie to be really convincing, it has to sound like it's true, and for a lie to sound true, it must have a background story. To make somebody act like a chicken, you need to have a pretty good background story, so how about this …

To fool one of your friends into doing a chicken impression, first you need to recruit two or three of your other pals. When you are standing together ~~and your victim~~ (actually, victim's not a nice word, is it, so we'll call him 'Humphrey') and Humphrey approaches, get your friends to start breathing heavily and holding their sides as though they are totally puffed out. Then, when Humphrey gets within earshot, say, 'I told you that none of you would be able to do it!' Humphrey will want to know what it is that no one can do, so when he asks what's going on, tell him the following tale.

Fantastic Fact or Fab Fib?

If you tell a lie in a court of law, after having sworn to tell the truth, you are committing a crime called perjury and can be prosecuted.

On Sunday you were visiting your aunt's house and your mum and dad made you walk there the long way round so that they could look at the gravestones in the churchyard/flowers in the park/fish in the pond (whatever seems most believable). When you were on your way home, your dad played a trick on you. He said you could either walk home the way you had come or take the quicker route. You, of course, opted for the quicker route – you'd been moaning about not having come in the car in the first place. So your dad said, 'Okay, we'll take the quick route if you can say "Quick walk back" really fast.' You said it, simple enough, but then he challenged you to say it ten times really quickly using just one breath and saying the word 'back' really loud. Also, to make sure that you couldn't take an extra-deep breath, you had to stuff your fists into your armpits to stop your chest expanding too much. That was when you discovered that nobody in the whole world can say 'Quick walk back' ten times, really fast, shouting the word 'back', with their fists stuffed in their armpits.

Humphrey will listen to all of this and, because it sounds like an easy challenge, he will have a go. He will stick his fists in his armpits and start reciting, 'Quick-walk-BACK! Quick-walk-BACK! Quick-walk-BACK!'

At that point you can stop him and say, 'Yeah, nobody in the world can say it – without doing a chicken impression!'

Fantastic Fact or Fab Fib?

A man once spent two weeks in London Zoo in the 1960s dressed as a seal. The other seals got along with him so well that, when he left, they became depressed and refused to eat.

How to Sneak Downstairs Without Waking Your Parents

Parents can be pretty harsh when it comes to making sure that you go to bed at a certain time and you stay there. They say they have your best interests at heart, and that's probably true, but it doesn't alter the fact that there are countless reasons why you might need to be downstairs wide awake when they think you should be upstairs sound asleep. Maybe there's a late-night movie on TV that you're desperate to see (keep that volume low); or football, or the Olympics, or a live concert from the other side of the world to watch. If your games console is downstairs you might have to take part in a late-night internet gaming session with your mates, or maybe you just want to raid the fridge. Well, once your parents are in bed, there's nothing stopping you, is there?

Nothing except your parents, that is.

When they are asleep, parents have superpower night hearing that means they can pick up the sound of the quietest light switch click, or the slightest door squeak, or the tiniest floorboard creak, or the heartbeat of an ant, from anywhere in the house, even through their closed bedroom door. Okay, maybe not the ant! But to get past them, you have to plan ahead.

Fantastic Fact or Fab Fib?

Melvyn Switzer from Kent, England, snored so loudly that he set a world record. He snored at ninety-two decibels, which was louder than having a truck driving through the room.

First of all, you need to know that they really are asleep. You could try bugging their room using an old baby monitor, but they are quite likely to find something like that and then your plan is scuppered before you've started. Even if you could actually hear one of them snoring away via a baby monitor bug, there's no guarantee that the other one isn't wide awake, reading one of those brick-thick books they keep on the bedside table. All you can do is wait until a long time after they have gone to bed before you make your move. Give it at least an hour. Set your phone on a silent 'vibrate' alarm and keep it by your pillow to wake you in case you nod off yourself.

Long before either you or your parents have gone to bed, however, you must have planned your operation in meticulous detail. First of all, you need to be able to see where you are going. Switching on a light may not be an option. The light switch might be practically silent but a sudden light beaming across the floor under your parents' bedroom door could easily betray you. You have to use any available natural light if you can. One evening (before you're meant to be in bed) try switching off your bedroom light to see how much moonlight or, better still, streetlight – far more reliable than moonlight – comes into the room. You can then work out how to leave your curtains open a little to let in enough light for you to find your bedroom door without tripping over all that stuff you leave lying around on the floor.

You will have the same problem outside your bedroom, so do the same thing. Work out if you can leave the curtains in the corridor open a crack to let in some light. If you can't get enough light from outside to let you see where you're going, you may have to use a torch. Unfortunately, most torches throw out a wide beam that will illuminate the whole corridor and flash under your parents' door just like the ceiling light, so you may have to narrow the beam. Lay your torch on a sheet of thin card and roll it so that you create a card 'tube' sticking out over the front of the torch. Tape this in place and it will narrow the torch beam. You can stifle the beam still further by placing your hand over the end of the tube and letting just a little light out through your fingers.

Fantastic Fact or Fab Fib?

In Milan, Italy, in 1972, a cinema usher was arrested for clicking his torch on and off during a screening of *The Godfather*. He used the flashes to hypnotise members of the audience and would then steal their wallets and handbags.

So, now you can see where you are going after lights-out, your next problem is to make your journey downstairs a silent one. What is going to make a noise? Obviously, you must not be carrying anything that clinks or jingles – no jewellery, hard plastic DVD cases or games controls that might clunk together. Hide anything like that – stuff you might need – downstairs beforehand. Don't wear shoes or slippers or socks. Shoes clump on floors and slippers or socks shuffle on carpets. Bare feet are quietest on carpets and most other surfaces. You should carry one sock with you, tucked into a pocket or somewhere that you can reach it quickly. When you are in bare feet, if you stub your toe on a banister or skirting board, you will have a split second while the 'OUCH!' message travels from the accident site in your toe all the way up to your brain. When it reaches your brain, you will feel the pain. Use that split second to grab your sock and stuff it in your mouth to muffle the whimpering. Make sure it's a clean one!

Once you are sure that YOU don't make any unwanted noises,

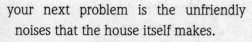

your next problem is the unfriendly noises that the house itself makes.

The squeaking of a door's hinges is something that sleeping parents' superhearing is fine-tuned to detect. Test all of the doors on your route beforehand, during the daytime, and squirt a tiny amount of oil on squeaky hinges. If you can't get your hands on a general purpose oil, then you can try a little bit of cooking oil or even some washing up liquid. Remember, all you need is a drop or two – you don't want a puddle of oil forming under the door and angry parents asking awkward questions. They're never going to believe that you were just trying to help out with a little DIY. After putting a couple of drops at the top of each door hinge, swing the door to and fro to let the oil get into the moving parts to lubricate them and eliminate the squeak.

Fantastic Fact or Fab Fib?

There are seven bones in the human ear that transmit vibrations from sound waves to our brain, which then interprets the signals. The bones are called the hammer, the anvil, the stirrup, the flange, the grommet, the biscuit and the plin.

Once you are sorted and the doors are sorted, your next noisy enemy is the floor. At night, floorboards come alive, creaking and groaning the moment you step on them as though you weighed as much as a blue whale (the largest creature that has ever lived, one hundred and seventy tonnes – always a handy fact to know), although it's unlikely that one of them has ever tried to sneak downstairs in your house at the dead of night. In fact, the floorboards creak just as much during the day. You don't notice it because there is so much other background noise going on.

What you have to do is find those creaks in the daytime and make a careful note of where they happen.

You need to create a 'creak map' of your route downstairs so that you know, for example, when you have taken three paces from your bedroom door, there is a creaky board and you have to take a giant step to get past it. There may be creaky steps on the stairs that you have to miss out, too. Mark the danger areas on your map and try to memorise them as it won't be easy to see at night, even by the light of your shaded torch.

After you have made it safely downstairs, and stayed as quiet as a mouse (a dead mouse – you don't get much quieter than that), you will have to retrace your steps back to bed using your creak map. Be very careful. After all that hard work, there's no point in getting busted on your way back to bed, is there?

Fantastic Fact or Fab Fib?

Young people grow most when they are sleeping and anyone under the age of eighteen who gets less than eight hours' sleep per night over a five-week period will start to shrink.

How to Get Out of Eating Foreign Muck on Holiday

When you go on the annual family holiday, or any trip with your parents, they will almost certainly try to make you eat things that you would never touch with a ten-foot pole at home, let alone with a fork and knife or, perish the thought, your fingers.

They just don't seem to understand that there are some foods that normal, sane kids like yourself will simply never want to eat. 'Why don't you try something different for a change?' they will say (probably again and again for days on end). What parents can't see is that when you go on holiday, there are a million things to do that are a million times better than sitting at a dining table while they force you to talk to them.

There will probably be arcade games somewhere close by

that you haven't tried at home; almost certainly a TV with weird foreign channels to laugh at or, better still, all the same channels that you like at home. Of course, you will probably have a games console with you, or be able to play games on your phone, but the parents will always want to drag you into a restaurant and make you put it away just when you're about to move up a level.

Even if you do actually want to sit down and eat, why on earth would you want to eat foreign stuff? Why can't they just let you eat the sort of things you enjoy at home? Why can't you have proper British food like burgers (which are actually German – 'burger' is short for Hamburger and named after Hamburg in Germany), or pizza (which is actually Italian), or sausages (which were made by the ancient Greeks and Romans), or chips (Belgian or French – they've been fighting over who invented them for centuries)?

Fantastic Fact or Fab Fib?

Because fish do not have fingers, fish fingers are actually made from their toes.

Instead, there are local things your parents will want you to try. In Greece, it might be moussaka, which is made with minced meat (and if it's minced, you've no way of knowing what it used to be), slimy vegetables called aubergines and a topping of blubbery white sauce. Yum! In Spain it could be paella, which can have pretty much anything in it, from unidentifiable shellfish with more legs and claws than an alien invasion, to roughly chopped bits of what was once a fluffy little bunny rabbit. Mainly, though, paella is a mountain of stodgy rice. Double yum! In France, they really do eat snails and frogs' legs but even the cruellest of parents won't actually want you to try them, so you should insist on ordering them – and a double helping for your younger sibling! You might skip the snails and frogs but be careful of French sausages, too, because some particularly repulsive types are made using cow and pig intestines and have a very peculiar smell. Triple yum!

So, foreign food is not to be trusted but how can you actually get out of eating it? What you must do is go armed with facts. Any true Naughty Kid should be able to make up a shedload of facts to back up any argument. These will all be lies but because you have been practising hard (you *have* been practising telling good lies, haven't you?) they will sound horrifically true. In the case of the food industry, however, you don't need to lie – the truth really is horrific enough.

Any of you who have had food hygiene or food science lessons at school, and paid the slightest attention, will know how dangerous food sounds: use that knowledge. When you are walking through the holiday resort, perhaps on your way back from the beach, and your parents stop to look in a restaurant where you can see the chef chopping up meat, they might mention that it would be nice to eat there instead of having burgers again.

That's when you say, 'We learned in school that an average kitchen chopping board has around 200 per cent more faecal bacteria on it than a toilet seat.' That's a horrifying FACT, and if you don't know what 'faecal' means, take a deep breath, steel yourself, and look it up in a dictionary.

Fantastic Fact or Fab Fib?

The Greek writer Homer, born around 2,700 years ago, wrote about a kind of sausage in his epic poem, *The Odyssey*.

If you are passing a restaurant where there is food on display in a cabinet, all laid out ready to be cooked to order, and your parents start to show an interest, just say, 'We learned in school that raw meat and poultry are breeding grounds for campylobacter, clostridium and E. coli bacteria, as well as salmonella [FACT], even when stored in ideal conditions, so what chance has this lot got, sitting near the street?'

In a hotel or restaurant where there is food in hot cabinets, either for self service or to be dished out by the staff, and your parents are trying to make you choose something weirdly foreign, just say, 'We learned in school that this stuff needs to be kept at a minimum of sixty-three degrees Celsius to prevent the development of the bacteria that cause food poisoning [FACT]. Does it seem that hot to you?' Of course, your parents won't have a clue what temperature the hot cabinet is, but by now you will be starting to sound pretty annoying to them. Well, what do they expect? They're the ones who are always telling you to pay attention at school, after all, and these are properly useful things to have learned.

The above are real facts, but you can invent your own, as long as you make sure they sound convincing. Facts that include statistics such as a percentage figure, or scientific/technical terms, will always sound more believable.

If all else fails and you are forced to eat something that you didn't want to eat, in a restaurant where you didn't want to be, then wait until later that night and try a holiday version of the vomiting trick that is described in 'How to Get Out of Sitting in the Middle' (page 42). You won't need to do any acting, because you can claim to have been sick in the night. Obviously, you will need to provide evidence of this and, because you were feeling too ill to make it to the loo, that evidence will be on the floor of your room.

To make a holiday vomit look convincing, plan in advance. Take a handful of freezer food bags on holiday with you. When you are sitting at the table, sneak a few spoons of whatever you are eating into the freezer bag and hide it in your pocket. It may be that your parents are keeping a close eye on you to make sure that you eat whatever muck has been put in front of you. In that case, once you have had a few bites to eat, ask to be excused so that you can go to the loo. Say something like, 'You know, this isn't as bad as I thought it would be', and take a big mouthful of the food as you get up from the table. Don't eat it, don't chew it, keep it in your mouth until you get to the loo and then spit it into your freezer bag.

Later, you need to add a bit of water to the mix and, when you are back in your room in the middle of the night, do your best, noisiest vomiting impression (just in case anyone might hear you) and dump the contents of the bag onto the floor. The food will still be recognisable as the stuff you ate earlier and this should be enough to get you out of ever having to eat there again.

Fantastic Fact or Fab Fib?

More than 50 per cent of raw chicken contains bacteria that cause more illnesses than salmonella.

How to Convince Your Younger Sibling Their Room is Haunted

Little brothers and sisters are always doing things that drive you totally nuts. They take your stuff without asking (not that you'd let them have any of your stuff, even if they DID ask); they are forever telling tales to get you into trouble; they laugh at you and make you look like an idiot every chance they get; they are constantly trying to hang out with you and your mates ... the list of things that they do goes on and on.

Everything on that list is crying out for payback – you need REVENGE – and that takes careful planning. It's not nice to plot and scheme against your own family, but being a nice kid isn't what this book is all about, is it? This is *The Naughty Kid's Handbook* and if you have any ideas about being nice to your sisters or brothers, then read no further – this book is not for you.

There is no better way of getting back at your younger sibling than scaring him or her witless. We're not talking about sneaking up behind them and bursting a paper bag or dropping a few spiders in their schoolbag. Those pranks are too easy, although you shouldn't discount them completely because they are still good for a laugh. No, we're talking about a major fright fest – something that will make their hair stand on end, their knees go wobbly and their socks burst into flames. What better way to achieve this than to make them think that their bedroom is haunted?

To make this work requires a lot of preparation and a good deal of effort but it will be worth it. If you can pull it off you are guaranteed a drastic outcome. And if they're really scared, you may even be ordered to swap rooms. If you have always wanted that room, of course, or just fancy a change, so much the better. You can make yourself look like a hero by agreeing to give up your room and move into the 'haunted' one. What you must *not* do, however, is volunteer to do that: it mustn't seem that swapping rooms is your idea because that could look a bit suspicious and get you into a whole heap of trouble.

So how do you go about persuading your sibling that his or her room is haunted? Well, just like all good lies, it has to have a really good story to back it up if anyone is ever going to believe it. You need to start with the background story and for that you must use your computer skills to create and print out a fake local history society newsletter – the sort of thing that comes through the letterbox and usually goes from the doormat to the dustbin in the blink of an eye, thrown out with the rest of the junk mail. To avoid that happening, you need to have a big photograph of your house on the newsletter. Whether your sibling or your parents pick it up off the doormat, where it will be lying on top of the usual pile of pizza delivery menus and other less useful advertising rubbish, the photo of your house will make them want to read it.

Of course, the newsletter will be on top of the rubbish lying behind the door because you put it there, carefully planting it when no one else was around so that no one knows it was your handiwork. Why is this newsletter so important? Because it will establish the background to your ghost story.

Fantastic Fact or Fab Fib?

Dogs and cats sitting sleeping peacefully in a room will waken, get up and leave when they sense that a ghost has entered.

You will have to give the newsletter an official-looking heading that reads: THE NEWTON (or whatever the name of your town or district is) LOCAL HISTORY SOCIETY and dress it up with some sort of a crest or logo.

Then, below the big picture of your house, which you should be able to take using your phone, you need to have a headline that reads: **The Sad Case of Maggie Chase**. The idea is that someone called Maggie Chase used to live in your house. She is going to be your ghost. If you live in an older house, then you won't have a problem with spinning this yarn about the old lady who lived in the property years before your family moved in. If you live in a modern house, then you will need to adapt the story by saying that Maggie's cottage used to be where your house now stands but was demolished to make way for the new housing. Adapting the story to make it fit your circumstances might need a bit of imagination, but needn't alter the basic story that appears on the news sheet, which goes as follows:

This house in Broomfield Road [your address needs to go here] was once the home of a woman named Maggie Chase. Maggie lived in Newton [your town or district goes here] all of her life and was a familiar sight to many when she was out shopping, always dressed in black, although she seldom spoke more than a few words to anyone she met. Maggie died in 1972, a sad and lonely old lady, but she hadn't always been such a forlorn figure.

In the 1920s, when Maggie was still a young woman, she first moved into Broomfield Road with her husband, Tom – a newly married couple. Maggie and Tom were both keen gardeners, growing award-winning flowers and even supplying blooms to be sold by a local florist. The couple had three sons, Charles, Henry and Thomas. It was shortly after Thomas was born that tragedy first struck the Chase family. Tom, who worked as a railway engineer, was killed in an accident. Without his wages, times were very hard for Maggie and her boys, but she took work as a cleaner, and as a gardener, and continued to sell cut flowers to the shop.

The boys used to gather petals from flowers in the garden, especially the roses, and use them to make a scent, giving their mother a fresh bottle of their home-made perfume every year for Christmas.

By the time the boys had grown into young men, the Second World War was raging and they were all drafted into the armed forces. Charles joined the Royal Navy, Henry went into the Army and Thomas served in the RAF. Tragically, none of them was to survive the war. Maggie was driven mad with grief and from then on was never seen wearing anything other than black, mourning her lost boys for the rest of her life.

Maggie had no other relatives and when she died, the house began to fall into disrepair. Eventually, it was taken over by the local council, who sent in workmen to clear the house and carry out essential repairs. Several of the workmen had strange experiences in the house. They reported feeling as though they were being watched, as if someone was in the room with them, and smelling a strange perfume in the bedroom at the back of the house [or wherever your sibling's room is], which had once been Maggie's bedroom. Two of the men, who claimed to have seen a figure dressed in black and to have heard the words

'Get out' being whispered, walked off the premises and refused ever to go back into the house. Maggie, it seemed, did not take kindly to having strangers in her house and had returned from the grave to expel the intruders.

There have been no reports of any sightings of Maggie since the refurbishment of the house [or new houses built on the site, depending on your version of the story] so hopefully Maggie is now at rest and reunited with her family.

That is the basic story that you can adapt to suit your own house. No doubt, when your fake newsletter is found, having apparently been delivered, the story will become a real talking point in your house. When you are sure that your sibling knows the story, you can start the haunting.

The first stage of the haunting should be quite mild. Sneak into your sibling's room when no one is around, and move a few things. Maybe you can move a hairbrush from wherever it normally sits and leave it on the window ledge or take a book that is by the bed and put it under a pillow. You should move little things to begin with, building up over a few days, whenever you get the chance. When you see hauntings happening in movies, things are hurled across rooms and there are some pretty impressive breakages. Don't damage anything, just move things. You will almost certainly be blamed if anything gets smashed up. Eventually, if you can get enough time in the house on your own, you could try re-arranging the whole room, moving the bed and any other furniture to different positions.

Once you start your haunting, you are bound to fall under suspicion and it may become very difficult to get into your sibling's room without being spotted. Be patient. Persuading your brother or sister that their room is haunted could take quite a long time but the next stage is worth waiting for – Maggie's perfume. What you need to do is give your sibling a whiff of perfume when they go to bed and you can do that using an old tennis ball and a straw.

Fantastic Fact or Fab Fib?

A house in the rue des Artistes in the famous artists' quarter of Paris is haunted by no fewer than seventeen ghosts, including the French painter Toulouse Lautrec. Lautrec was a short man and his ghost is said to dart around under the dinner table, kicking guests in the shins.

You need to puncture the tennis ball using a pair of scissors. The best way to do this is to put the ball on the ground and stand with your feet either side of it to hold it steady. Then gently push one of the blades of the scissors into the ball. BE REALLY CAREFUL DOING THIS: you don't want to cut yourself open, bleed to death and end up haunting the house for real!

Push a plastic straw in through the hole and then get your hands on some scent. You might want to invest in a small, cheap bottle of some sort of flowery perfume (you won't need much, just a few drops ought to do it). Dribble the perfume down the straw so that some of it ends up in the tennis ball. Then, plant the tennis ball under your sibling's mattress, with the straw poking out somewhere near the top of the bed where it won't be noticed. When your brother or sister gets into bed, the tennis ball will be squeezed and some of the scent will be puffed out through the plastic straw, to leave a faint smell of perfume in the air.

You will have to remove the tennis ball before the sheets on the bed are changed because it would definitely be discovered. Once the sheets have been changed, of course, you can always put it back again. If a trace of perfume doesn't make your sibling think that Maggie has returned, then you need to try something a bit less subtle.

Most people have a regular routine when they go for a shower or a bath and you will doubtless know when your sibling does so. Annoying little siblings always spend far longer than anyone else in the bathroom. You have to get into the bathroom just before he or she takes a shower. Then, using nothing but your finger, write the words GET OUT! on the bathroom mirror. You shouldn't be able to see what you have written but when the bathroom gets steamy from the hot water and the mirror steams up, the words GET OUT! will appear on the steamed-up mirror. That should be enough to freak out your sibling completely.

For your haunting to be successful, you have to use real stealth. You can't afford to be spotted setting up any of your stunts. Stealth and secrecy are essential for a successful haunting, so no one will ever know it was you.

Fantastic Fact or Fab Fib?

The White House in Washington, home to the President of the United States, is said to be haunted by several ghosts, including Abigail Adams (wife of the country's second President, John Adams), former President Abraham Lincoln and a certain Mr Burns, who once owned the land on which the White House is built.

How to Get Out of Sitting Next to the Nutter on the Bus

We've all been there. There's only one seat left on the bus and the person sitting window-side is well known to you – notorious among all of your friends. He's the weirdo who will start talking as soon as you sit down and won't give up until you've heard all about his collection of toe-nail clippings, how he trained as a cosmonaut at a secret Russian base just outside Stoke-on-Trent, and the best way to photograph a cabbage using only a cornflakes box and a piece of Elastoplast. And, strangely, he actually smells a bit of cabbage. Always.

Meanwhile, your mates will be laughing their socks off because they're the ones taking up all the other seats. They managed to avoid the nutter and left him to you.

The nutter is always on the bus somewhere. How he manages always to be in place, no matter which bus stop you and your mates choose, no matter which day it is, no matter what the weather, is a complete mystery. But he is always there, nevertheless. So how do you avoid him?

Normally, when you're in the crush to get on the bus, everyone just wants to push ahead and grab a seat. But you have to be smarter than that; you have to keep your wits about you. When you see the bus coming, try to gauge how full it is. If it looks as if there are lots of seats, then you have nothing to worry about; you'll have plenty of choice and you can probably have a double seat to yourself if you want. On the other hand, if the bus is crowded, there will be very little choice, so you have to have a plan.

Fantastic Fact or Fab Fib?

Queue (the kind you stand in waiting at a bus stop) and cue (the kind that men in fancy waistcoats use to play snooker) may be spelt differently but they sound the same. Such words are called homophones.

You do not want to be the first one on. You might think being first will give you the best choice of seats, but you must never forget what it's like if the nutter catches your eye when you're scrambling towards a seat. Nutters are like people magnets: once they have made eye contact, they can draw you towards them whether you want to go or not. Once they've fixed you with their 'Hello, my name's Julius Caesar' stare, they can reel you in like a fish on a line, so you do not want to be first on. If you find yourself at the front of the queue, pretend to drop something and then bend to pick it up; someone else is bound to skip in front of you. They think they've been smart, but now they're first in line for the nutter.

Once on board, you have to be eagle-eyed. Look for a seat, but keep a sharp eye out for you-know-who. If you are behind one of your mates and you spot the dreaded nutter, act as if you are being hustled by the crowd behind and gently force your mate towards him. You can even use your pal as a human shield to let you sneak past and grab a seat in a nutter-free zone.

All of this means that you have to be constantly aware and alert, which can be really exhausting, especially after a hard day of dodging work at school, but if you are no good at manipulating everyone else to make sure that you don't have to sit beside the nutter, then you are going to end up with him day after day. If that's the case, or if you simply want to make sure that you always get a double seat all to yourself, then there's only one thing to do – become the nutter. You can turn yourself into the person that no one wants to sit next to!

> ### Fantastic Fact or Fab Fib?
>
> In the 1960s a group of hippies set out to travel from England to India in a three-wheeled bus they decided to call 'Mystic Journey'. In fact, they spelt it incorrectly and painted 'Mistake Journey' on the side of their bus. It broke down after just 4.8 kilometres (3 miles) and they gave up.

Becoming a nutter could either make you very unpopular, or a school legend. Whatever happens, once you go down this route there is no turning back, but it is the naughtiest way by far and this book is all about the art of naughtiness, after all. It may be that all you have to do to get strangers, other schoolkids or even the actual nutter to think that you are best avoided is to glance sideways at anyone who sits next to you and start talking complete rubbish – 'My granny drives a Zeppelin shaped like a hedgehog' or 'I can hold my breath until my ears bleed' or 'Do you want to share my lunch?'

That last one may not sound too strange, but you will have prepared in advance. What you need is a small plastic bag – a freezer food bag is ideal. Then you chew up half a Mars Bar. Eat the other half – there's no point in wasting a whole, perfectly good Mars Bar! Put the chewed-up chocolate into the freezer bag and then tuck it inside the waistband of your trousers, at the side, towards the back. When you're on the bus and you say, 'Do you want to share my lunch?' you make a big show of sticking your hand down your trousers and pulling out a handful of gooey brown stuff. 'I ate it yesterday.'

Well, would you want to sit next to a kid who did that?

Fantastic Fact or Fab Fib?

Falling asleep on a public bus is a criminal offence in seven states in America and is punishable by being sent to prison for up to ten days.

How to Win
at Rock, Paper,
Scissors

Rock, paper, scissors is one of the most frustrating games in the world, guaranteed to cause more disputes than it solves. Even if they decided to use it as a way of settling debates at the United Nations, if the Chinese lost they would be shouting, 'No – best of three!' and if the Americans then lost they would be shouting, 'No – best of five!' And so it would go on, just as it does in school playgrounds and bike sheds everywhere.

It may not be the way to settle international disputes, but that's no reason for you ever to lose at rock, paper, scissors, which, from now on, we will call RPS. You can use RPS to settle all sorts of things from the classic car journey argument about who's going to sit in the middle (in case you haven't had a chance to prepare yourself by following the instructions in 'How to Get Out of Sitting in the Middle', page 42) to who gets the last chocolate in the box. You can try other methods of settling disputes, like tossing a coin or rolling dice, but YOU are not completely in control if you agree to that, and if a Naughty Kid is going to come out on top, being in control is essential. Unlike so many other contests, RPS is not a game of chance. If you work hard at it, you can take control. It involves skill, tactics and cunning.

The skill part comes in observation and execution; the tactics involve dominating your opponent and split-second decision making; and cunning ... well, that's just another word for cheating, isn't it? Yes, like every other game, the Naughty Kid's best option for winning – and we're always in it to win it, right? – is to CHEAT.

In order to perfect the art of breaking the rules at RPS, of course, you first have to know what those rules are, so let's quickly run through how the game is played.

You don't need any props, tools, or equipment to play RPS (unless you are planning to cheat), just a small space where you can stand with your opponent. Stand with your right hand behind your back and, on the count of three, you each whip your hand round in front of you, with your fingers making one of three signs. The rock is a clenched fist. Paper is a flat, open hand held palm-down. The scissors are a clenched fist with the forefinger and middle finger held out and separated like the blades of a pair of scissors.

Each of the signs can beat, or be beaten by, one of the others. Rock blunts scissors to win, but is wrapped in paper to lose. Paper wraps rock to win but loses to scissors, which can cut paper. Scissors, of course, cut paper but lose to rock.

These simple rules have made RPS a game that has been played for countless years around the world – not since the dawn of time, perhaps, but certainly since the dawn of scissors.

Fantastic Fact or Fab Fib?

Because the Chinese invented paper, you might think that rock, paper, scissors was first played in China, and you would be right – although it was played as 'slug, frog, snake'.

RPS has been studied by very clever people who have even developed robots that can play and beat human opponents. Such people earn handsome salaries for coming up with ideas like this and it is such a cool way to earn a living that they were undoubtedly Naughty Kids when they were younger. You don't, however, have to study engineering for years and build a robot to win at RPS; you just have to study your opponent for a couple of minutes, because research into RPS has shown that certain players are likely to play in certain, predictable ways.

Men and boys who are not experienced or regular players, for example, and have not studied tactics, will tend to start their first contest with rock. It seems that males think rock is the tough, clenched-fist option that shows they are strong, hard and tough. If you are playing someone like that, obviously you should start with paper.

When playing a beginner like this, move on swiftly to the next 'throw' without giving them time to think about tactics or their own game strategy. Not having had time to think, their instinct will probably be to copy the last winning throw, so they will go for paper. You play scissors ... and already you have won two out of three.

Inexperienced female opponents are less likely to play rock on their first throw, leaving you a 50/50 chance of predicting their move. You have to assess the individual to decide what they are likely to play. Scissors is the more aggressive move, likely to be played by someone you think is determined to win. Paper, despite the fact that it beats the mighty rock, is often seen as a defensive move and could well be played by a beginner who seems more timid.

Fantastic Fact or Fab Fib?

Paper is the least popular move in a game of rock, paper, scissors. Studies have shown that it is used around 30 per cent of the time while rock and scissors are each used around 35 per cent.

Experienced players who have some idea of tactics and strategy are likely to know all of this, so will play differently and are quite unpredictable. They may, however, look upon YOU as a beginner and you can take advantage of that, at least on your first throw. They will expect you to play the beginner's throws, so, if you are male, throw scissors instead of rock to win against their paper. If you are female, throw rock to win against scissors or draw against the opponent's rock, should they have somehow got the impression that you are out to win. Of course, if you act a little shy and uncertain, your opponent won't have a clue that you actually know what you are doing and have come into the game with a plan to win. You can even try putting on a wimpy act by saying things like, 'You won't actually hit my hand, will you? It's just that I bruise easily and I have to finish writing an essay about wild flowers later.'

If none of the above seems much like cheating to you, then you're right. These are legitimate tactics, although acting like a wimp is a bit underhand. Keeping your opponent guessing is all part of the RPS mind game. Serious players – and there are, of course, World Championships in RPS – will study other players to work out if there is any pattern to the throws they make or if they give away the move they are about to make with a particular facial expression. Nuts, isn't it? A serious player might also try to get you to play with your hand in plain sight instead of behind your back. In this game you pump your hand up and down three times together and then throw your hands. NEVER agree to this. Some players claim to be able to predict your throw by watching the way the muscles in your hand tense.

In an ordinary, everyday RPS battle, it's unlikely that you will come up against a player like that, but you should ALWAYS insist on starting with your hand behind your back. Why? Because it's the best way to cheat! What you have to do is to make sure that you are standing in front of a mirror, a shop window or a car window – any kind of reflective surface. Make sure that your opponent has his or her back to the reflector and, if you stand at the right angle, you should be able to see whether he or she is forming a rock, paper or scissors before the throw is even made. Check out suitable places beforehand to find the best spot to spy on the hand behind your opponent's back.

Your opponent might spot the reflector cheat, but there are plenty of other underhand ways to win. As your hands come round for the throw, look for what shape your opponent is throwing. You can't change the shape in mid-air – flapping your fingers about like a spider in a hurricane is definitely cheating and you should make a huge fuss about that if you see anyone doing that. Delaying your throw so that you can catch a glimpse for just an instant at what your opponent is doing is also cheating but you can angle your body slightly, with your free shoulder a little further forward, to disguise your moment's delay. You can also distract your opponent by using a martial-arts-style scream as you make your throw. Anything that gives you that split second to see what the other player is about to throw works in your favour.

Instead of a martial-arts scream as you make your move, you can put your opponent off even more by yelling 'ROCK!', 'PAPER!' or 'SCISSORS!' Of course, if you scream 'ROCK!' just as you are making your move, what you actually play is scissors. Your opponent will hear you shout and, if not already poised to play paper against you, he or she will become flustered and change halfway through the throw. You then need to pounce on that fluttery hand change and claim the game because your opponent was cheating. If the other player plays paper you win, and you also win if they try to change to paper.

There is another hugely annoying tactic that you can use to upset your opponent. If you both play rocks, instead of counting it as a draw, immediately stick up your thumb and call, 'BOOM! Dynamite blows your rock to bits!' You can try to claim that dynamite will, in fact, beat anything. You're not likely to get away with that, but it might help to put other players off their game. Should anybody be daft enough to accept that a losing throw can be turned into dynamite, make sure that when you throw a winner you whip your hand out of the way again quickly so that you can't be blown to pieces.

You may win using these tricks, but it may also happen that other players will become so fed up with you that they won't play you any more. That's fine. If you win and no one will play against you, you can declare yourself the undefeated champion!

Fantastic Fact or Fab Fib?

In Madrid in 2003, French RPS fanatic Jacques l'Esparrow played a marathon seven-hour game against the Spanish National Champion, Campo Viejo. The Frenchman struggled on in great pain for the last three hours after he threw a hugely enthusiastic rock and broke his wrist. The Spaniard won 3,513–3,511.

How to Get
Out of Games
and PE

When you're at school in the winter, sitting in a perfectly warm, dry classroom having a chat with your mates when the teachers think you're working; or secretly sending texts on the phone they say you're not meant to be using; or finding ways to access games that they don't want you to play on the school computer, the thought of being sent out onto the cold, damp playing fields for 'games' can send a shiver down your spine.

Why do they insist that you have to play football or hockey or rugby and get soaked to the skin and covered in mud? Don't they understand that the best place for sport is on the telly? Of course, some kids actually enjoy going outside and running around, and good luck to them, but if you really want to be considered a Naughty Kid, then you need to find a way out of the games lessons at school. PE is no better. It may be indoors, but running around in a gym hall getting hot and sweaty is almost as bad as the football, hockey or rugby and getting drenched. Nothing, however, is as bad as those frosty, bitingly cold days when you are sent off on the much-despised cross-country run. Let's face it, if kids were meant to run for miles outside in the freezing cold, no one would ever have invented parents with warm, comfy cars.

And the worst thing is that when the teachers send you out in the freezing cold, they make you wear LESS than you had on in the centrally heated classroom. Shorts and T-shirts – in the middle of winter! It's madness! Every Naughty Kid needs to know how to get out of doing games.

Fantastic Fact or Fab Fib?

Rugby was invented at Eton school when a boy called Henry Webb Ellis was playing football with a bunch of other lads. It was his ball and he had to go home for tea so he picked it up and ran off the pitch, shoving people out of the way as he went.

The usual excuses – 'Forgot my games kit', 'Didn't realise it was on Wednesdays this term' or 'Somebody stole my shorts last week' – will only earn you a detention or the embarrassment of running around in a pair of filthy shorts that are ten sizes too big and have been rotting away in the lost property box since last century. As a Naughty Kid, you need to be a lot more creative than that.

You could use the 'How to Get Out of Gardening' hay fever scam (page 59). It will work in summer to get you out of sports but can also work in winter as a heavy cold. Obviously, the hay fever excuse may be used from time to time in the summer months, but you can't use it too often as a 'cold' in the winter without somebody getting a bit suspicious. What you really need is something like hay fever that you can bring into play reasonably regularly during the winter. Eczema is the answer.

Eczema is a nasty skin condition that afflicts millions of people and you wouldn't wish it on your worst enemy – truly. It causes dry, itchy skin, rashes and cracking or flaking of the skin – all very uncomfortable and sometimes unbearably painful. It can be made worse by exercise, especially if it affects the skin on the knees or in areas where there will be lots of bending and flexing. Only a complete psychopath would make someone with eczema do games and, while your games teacher may well fall into that category, he or she won't dare send you out in the cold with eczema on your knee. The thought of letters of complaint arriving at the school and the whole quagmire of regulations in the 'Health and Safety' area as well as the fact that your teachers have a duty of care towards their pupils – they have to make sure you are safe and that you don't do anything that might result in you coming to any harm – all mean that nobody will make a kid with eczema do sports. Of course, unless you are unfortunate enough actually to suffer from eczema, you can't use it as a way of getting out of games lessons or PE. What you have to do is to make your teacher believe that you have eczema. So how do you fake this horrible condition?

As always for any successful dodge, thorough preparation is the key. You will need make-up or face paints, a little ordinary flour, a saucer, some water and a fork (the kind you eat sausages with, not the gardening kind).

Practise creating your eczema a couple of times before you try to pass it off as the real thing. Getting the colour and the textures right is the key to making it look good (or rather, really bad) and the temptation at first will always be to use too much.

What you must do is to create a patch of redness on your knee that looks sore, like a rash. A little blusher make-up or pinkish face paint ought to do the trick. While that is drying nicely, take just a teaspoon of flour and put it in the saucer. Add a dribble of water and mix well with the fork until you have a smooth paste, something like the consistency of toothpaste.

Fantastic Fact or Fab Fib?
Research over a fifteen-year period at Lancaster University has shown that children who enjoy taking part in four or more different sports are far more likely to grow up to be really annoying.

Use the fork to scrape a little of the mixture onto your knee on top of the 'rash'. Spread it thinly over the whole area of the rash but don't worry if it is a little bit thicker in some places. Now you have to wait for it to dry, and that may take fifteen or twenty minutes, so be patient.

When the flour-and-water paste is dry, the thinnest areas will look white, like flaky skin, with the pink 'rash' showing through from underneath. Where it is a bit thicker, the paste will be hard and will crack like painfully cracked skin.

Your fake eczema will stick to your leg all day underneath your trousers and when it comes to the games lesson, you can put on a slight limp and tell the teacher that you are having a bit of an eczema problem. You didn't get a note from your mum or dad because it didn't seem so bad earlier on that morning, but now there's no way you can run around. Roll up your trouser leg to show off your handiwork. You can even rub it a bit round the edges where it is thinnest and it will flake off like dry skin dandruff.

The good thing about eczema – especially good for those who really do suffer from it – is that in most cases it can be treated and kept under control but, a bit like hay fever, certain things can bring it on unexpectedly. Allergies, different kinds of foods, the weather, central heating or even clothes washed using a different soap can all cause a flare-up. You can, therefore, get away with faking eczema to get out of games but have 'recovered' in a day or two so that you don't have to go limping around the school all the time.

The only drawback with the flour-and-water paste on your knee is getting rid of it. It sticks there really well but you can enjoy some quiet time in your room picking it off with your fingernails. It's almost as satisfying as picking scabs but without the pain and the blood!

Speaking of pain and blood, the flour-and-water paste can be used to make cracked skin and wounds on your face as well as your knees if you ever need to dress up as a zombie. You can mix a few drops of face paint in with the water when making it to create really horrible effects from the realm of the walking dead. Well, we all like to dress as a zombie from time to time, don't we? Apart from anything else, and if all of your efforts to get out of it failed, looking like a zombie would be a great way to come staggering back from the dreaded cross-country run!

Fantastic Fact or Fab Fib?

There are more than 100 countries in the official Rugby Union world rankings, including Uzbekistan at number 96 and New Zealand at number 1. The first Rugby World Cup was won by New Zealand in 1987.

How to Make it Look Like You've Had a Shower at School Without Actually Having Had One

If nothing that you could think of has worked; if no one believes that you are too poorly for games or PE; if the school has emailed your parents to check that you don't have eczema or a rare form of sleeping sickness that means you must lie down in a warm, comfortable room instead of taking exercise; if you have been forced to run around in the fresh air and get a bit sweaty and muddy ... the next horror that you will have to face is when the games teacher expects you to have a shower.

There's nothing wrong with having a shower. It can be quite pleasant standing under the hot water listening to music at home in your own bathroom in comfort and privacy. On the other hand, when there's only a pathetic sprinkle of lukewarm water trickling out of the shower head and you're in a shower room that's even more damp, muddy and disgusting than the changing rooms you have spent so much effort trying to avoid, a shower is not such a pleasant experience. You get wet and cold, it all feels pretty horrible – and there is certainly no privacy.

'What are you worried about?' the teachers will say. 'No one's interested in looking at you with no clothes on.' But that's not true, is it? You know that everyone else in the shower room will be looking at your private bits. Of course everyone sneaks a quick peek just to make sure that their bits are the same as everyone else's, because that's exactly what *you* do, too. Nevertheless, there is no point in going through all of that cold, damp, shower room misery if you can avoid it, and the best way to do that is to prepare in advance.

Fantastic Fact or Fab Fib?

Studies in Japan have shown that the pounding your head takes from water falling on it in a shower can cause baldness and brain damage.

If you suspect even for a moment that, despite giving a performance worthy of an Oscar, no one is going to believe that you are unfit for sport, then you have to make sure that you are ready to dodge the shower by packing the right kit in your bag. You will need two towels. One must be wide enough to cover your whole body from the armpits down to the knees – below the knees, if possible. The other can be smaller but has to be big enough to cover all of your hair and your shoulders as well, if possible. You will also need a bottle of water.

When you come in from the sports field or the PE hall, you will have to get changed out of your games kit – but instead of stripping off for a shower, as soon as you can do so without being spotted wrap your big towel around you, leaving your shorts secretly in place. Wrap the towel tight under your armpits and, before you tuck in the top of the free end to hold the towel in place, slip the bottle of water inside the towel so that you can hold it there by gripping it against your body with your arm. Drape your smaller towel over your shoulders and head off towards the showers. The towels will be keeping you well covered and reasonably warm.

On the way to the showers, pop into the loo. Get into a toilet cubicle and wait there for a couple of minutes, then take out the bottle of water and splash some water on your face. Not too much – the whole point of this exercise is to avoid getting cold and wet, after all. Leave the water bottle in the cubicle. You won't be able to carry it back in secret because you will now need both arms. Drape the small towel over your head, leaving just your water-splashed face showing. You can then head back towards the changing rooms.

Fantastic Fact or Fab Fib?

Having a shower is more eco-friendly than taking a bath because it uses less water. A shower may use between forty-five to ninety litres (ten and twenty gallons) of water, whereas a bath can use more than three times that amount.

As you are walking back, rub the towel on your head as though you are towelling your hair dry. Any teachers standing by to spot shower dodgers will see your wet face but they won't be able to spot that you are towelling perfectly dry hair. Neither will they be able to tell that the rest of you is bone dry, too.

Your next problem comes once you are back in the changing room. You can't just whip off your towel in case a teacher does happen to be passing and spots that you are still wearing your shorts and that you are totally dry. If you can fit your trousers (girls may have to be thinking about a skirt here) on over your shorts, then you now have to perform the sort of under-the-towel dressing manoeuvre normally seen only at the beach when someone is trying to swap a wet swimming costume for a dry one. If your trousers (or skirt) can't go over the shorts, then the shorts will have to go and it really does become like one of those beach-changing dances. Don't worry: practise a couple of times at home and you will be surprised how quickly you can do it.

Then, all you need to do is get back into the rest of your clothes and you will have avoided the cold, damp, miserable and embarrassing shower room experience – until next time. Of course, there is the possibility that you could get busted. If, for example, the tail end of your towel catches in a closing changing room door

and you carry on walking, leaving it behind, even the least observant teacher with the thickest glasses will be able to see that you haven't actually undressed properly.

If this happens, give a big smile, have a laugh and say, 'Nearly fooled you there, didn't I, Miss [or Sir]!' Make a joke of it and you might get away with being made to have a shower instead of being forced to run six times round a football pitch ... and then have a shower.

Fantastic Fact or Fab Fib?

At New York State University in Buffalo, Kevin 'Catfish' McCartney set a record for the longest ever shower, staying under the shower head for over three hundred and forty hours – that's more than two weeks!

How to Get Out of Being Blamed for a Fart on a Plane

When you think about it, so many people nowadays go on holiday by plane, or go on business trips by plane, or generally travel by air that it must have happened to almost everyone who has spent any length of time in a passenger jet: the unwanted fart.

You, of course, are not to blame since you have been forced to spend hours hanging around in an airport with nothing to do except eat crisps and burgers and drink fizzy drinks until it was time to board the plane. Well, that's bound to have an effect eventually, isn't it? The problem is that, in a plane, everyone is crammed in quite close together. You will probably find yourself sitting next to a complete stranger who is not going to be amused if you lift a leg or rock over onto one bum-cheek to let loose a real rip-snorter. What's more, you might be stuck sitting next to that person for another few hours, so you don't want to upset them, do you? Or *do* you?

Holding in a troublesome fart just to avoid upsetting the person sitting next to you is what a nice, thoughtful, delightful child would do – the sort of child who always makes his or her bed in the morning, never forgets to clean their teeth and always hands their homework in on time. That's not you. You are reading this book in order to learn how to pull the naughtiest stunts and get away with them – so what are your options when a rumbler down under starts bubbling?

Fantastic Fact or Fab Fib?

On average, a person (male or female) produces half a litre (0.8) of fart gas every day. On a four-hour flight in a plane carrying five hundred people, the air conditioning has to clear over forty litres (seventy pints) of farts.

That nice kid, the one who always makes the bed, etc., etc., etc., might say 'Excuse me' in the politest possible way, squeeze out of the seat and shuffle off in a clenchy-buttocked way to join the queue for the loo. But you're not going to do that. No Naughty Kid worth his or her salt will leave the movie they are watching just when it's started to get interesting and then climb past everyone else (naturally you will have wangled yourself a window seat) in order to stand in a loo queue while holding in gut eruptions that make Pompeii seem like the bursting of a snot bubble.

No – if you feel like letting one go mid-flight, then you don't have to struggle out of your seat and queue up just to do a bit of bum yodelling in the bog. A proper Naughty Kid will just trumpet away, but there's no point in taking the blame when there are so many other candidates in close proximity. So how do you get away with it?

The first thing to bear in mind is that you don't really have to worry about the noise. Planes are noisy places with the hissing of the air conditioning, the roar of the engines, the chit-chat of hundreds of people and the screaming of a few infants. In fact, if there's one of those close to where you are sitting, it can take the blame for pretty much everything. Many people will also be wearing earphones, either to enjoy the in-flight entertainment or to listen to their own music, which means they are not going to hear a thing, even if you squeeze one out that sounds like Godzilla blowing a raspberry. (There is a reason, by the way, why a raspberry is called a raspberry. It is rhyming slang and short for 'raspberry tart', which rhymes with … you guessed it.)

If you think it's at all possible that you might break wind with record-breaking volume, then you can probably cover it up with a couple of nicely timed coughs. The air that you breathe on a plane does give you a bit of a dry throat, after all.

No amount of coughing, however, can cover up what comes

next. If you've been playing your cards right in the airport, you will have had hot dogs, spicy pizza, burgers, chips and fizzy drinks that will produce enough gas to burst a Zeppelin – and you know it's not going to waft out smelling of roses. If you do have a very young child or an infant in nappies close by, then right at the moment when your nearest neighbours' eyes start to water, you too must act like you've just been hit with pepper spray. Others will be looking round to spot who to blame and you must do so as well, but then focus your gaze, with a disgusted frown, on the small child and anyone looking at you will be thrown off the scent, so to speak.

If there is no small child, then you will have to try another ploy. Reach up to the console above your seat and fumble with the air vent, then press the button to call the flight attendant. When he or she comes over, complain in a loud voice that there is a horrible smell coming out of your vent (which, in a way, is true). We all know that the air coming out of the vents is filtered clean and doesn't smell, but you are a kid and can act like you *don't* know that. Anyone sitting next to you will hear you complain about the smell coming from somewhere, and assume that, because you think it's coming from the vent, it can't be coming from you.

Fantastic Fact or Fab Fib?

A man in Kirkcaldy in Scotland adapted his motorbike to run on his own fart gas instead of petrol. He had to eat at least one curry and two tins of beans every day to keep his bike going.

If you don't fancy trying the vent routine, then you could also call the flight attendant over, wrinkle your nose and say, 'Have you started serving food or something?' In-flight meals always smell a bit farty, after all.

It may be, of course, that one of your family recognises the stench as being your particular brand. This needn't be a problem. The grown-ups will almost certainly go along with whatever ploy you attempt in order to avoid the embarrassment of being responsible for the kid who was responsible for stinking out the plane. If you have brothers or sisters, they can be more of a nuisance. They are likely to point straight at you and yell, 'That was *you*!' This is their downfall. There is an old saying about farts that goes along the lines of 'Who smelt it, dealt it', meaning that the first one claiming to smell a guff and attempting to blame someone else for the pong is almost certainly the person who dropped the clanger in the first place. If your brother or sister tries to pin the blame on you, stay calm, stare them right in the eye so that everyone can see, and say, 'No, I think that was *you*, wasn't it?'

Even if your sibling is not immediately branded a liar and blamed for the bottom burp, you will have created enough confusion to keep everyone guessing until it has all, quite literally, blown over.

Fantastic Fact or Fab Fib?

Dolphins can communicate over distances of up to sixteen kilometres (ten miles) underwater by farting. Scientists have analysed the messages they send, which appear to say, 'For goodness' sake, someone open a window!'

How to Win an Argument With Your Sister or Brother

*Y*ou know how it goes. There's a video game you both want to play, a hoodie you both want to wear or the last cake in the cupboard that you both want to eat … and the argument starts.

'You can't have that – it's mine!'

'Oh, yeah? Got your name on it, has it?'

'It was given to me.'

'I don't think so.'

'Yes, it was!'

'Oh, no, it wasn't …'

… and before you know it, you are into pantomime season with the 'Oh, yes, it is' and 'Oh, no, it isn't' see-saw argument that can go on for hours – or at least until a fight breaks out.

That, of course, is one way to settle the argument – fight it out – but it's not recommended. If you win, the loser will go crying to someone, sobbing, telling tales and probably getting lots of sympathy in return. Then you will be in deep doo-doo for having been a bully, even though you were only sticking up for yourself, like your parents always say you should. Whatever it was you were fighting over will probably be taken away from you into the bargain, unless you've already eaten it. That would be the cake, obviously, not the game or the hoodie.

Fantastic Fact or Fab Fib?

Harold and Margaret Evans of Springfield, Illinois, USA, bought their first television in 1962 and argued for twenty years about whose turn it was to get up out of their armchair to change the channel. The argument ended in 1982 when they bought a TV with a remote control but they divorced a month later after arguing about who should be in charge of the remote.

On the other hand, there is the possibility that you might LOSE a fight. Your brother or sister (let's just call them 'the enemy') may be bigger, tougher or simply a violent nutcase. Losing a fight is painful, humiliating and degrading, although it does give you a very good excuse to start plotting a lovely revenge campaign. Apart from that, there is really nothing positive to

be said for losing a fight or, indeed, for getting into the fight in the first place. That's what dimwits do; Naughty Kids know better. There is only one sure way of winning an argument, or anything else for that matter ... CHEAT!

How can you cheat at an argument? That's a tricky one, even for the most skilful of Naughty Kids. You can't really cheat in an argument where there are no rules. So, if you can't cheat in the argument, offer a fair way of settling the dispute ... and then cheat on the settlement. As a bonus, you can have a bit of fun into the bargain.

The settlement you should offer to resolve the argument is to choose cards from a pack. Offer the enemy the opportunity to pick a card and if you can guess which one it was once it has been hidden back in the pack again, you win. Naturally, you will have tampered with the pack beforehand to make sure that you do win, and here's how to do it.

Once again – you should be learning this by now –

137

preparation is key to pulling off a successful stunt. It may be that a pack of cards is kept in a drawer somewhere in your house. Perhaps there are two packs. If so, you can tamper with them both. The way you will rig the cards won't stop anyone else from using them normally at any other time, so you can have a rigged deck sitting in the drawer for weeks until you actually need it. You must, however, check that the deck is still in its 'doctored' state when you take it out of the drawer.

Fantastic Fact or Fab Fib?

If you add together the numbers on all of the cards in a pack, counting the ace as 1 and face cards as 10, the total is 365, the same as the number of days in the year.

To rig the pack, all you have to do is to take out all of the diamonds, arrange them in order from ace to king and then return them to the pack on the bottom. When you sit the pack face down on a table as a deck of cards, the bottom card should be the ace of diamonds. Next one up is the two, then the three and so on, until you reach the king. From there on up, the rest of the cards are a normal random selection.

Having checked that you still have diamonds at the bottom, fan the deck out in your hands, face down, keeping those diamonds off to one side and unfanned so that none of them is chosen. When the enemy chooses a card, you don't get to see it. Close up the fan into a deck again, put it on the table and then cut the cards. To do this you take roughly half of the cards off the top of the deck and put them on the table, still face down. Ask the enemy to put the chosen card on top of that pile, again face down. Now put the bottom pile on top to make one complete cut deck.

This is the clever bit. You know that the chosen card was on top of the cards that are now the bottom half of your deck. You also know that the ace of diamonds was on the bottom of the original deck. Because you put the original deck on top of the half that was separated, you now know that the ace of diamonds is sitting on top of the chosen card.

Now turn the deck over so that the bottom card is face up. Ask the enemy to cut the deck, as though you are mixing his or her card in even further. If the cut reveals a diamond, then complete the cut, take the deck and turn it face down. Should the cut not reveal a diamond, complete the cut and cut again. Cut and complete until a diamond shows up.

When a diamond is revealed, let's say that it's the seven, you know that on the bottom of the other stack there is a six, then a five, then a four, then a three, then a two, then the ace, then the chosen card. You complete the cut, pick up the deck and turn it over. Start dealing the cards, all now face down, counting in your head: six, five, four, three, two, one – BINGO! As you are dealing, say to the enemy, 'That's not yours, that's not yours, that's not yours', then pause when you count down to the chosen card. Say, 'I think that this might be it', then turn it over to reveal the card chosen by the enemy.

Try this trick a few times on your own for a bit of practice. It's a simple one to do and once you have gone through it a few times you will be able cheat the enemy with confidence, winning the argument.

Unless the enemy is particularly thick, he or she is not going to agree to settle any other argument this way, so best save the card trick for a major squabble that you really want to win. A wise Naughty Kid knows which battles to choose, so don't fight every argument. Let the little ones go and then, when you do choose to put up a proper fight, this easy card trick can be a very useful weapon in your armoury.

Fantastic Fact or Fab Fib?

The four 'suits' in a standard pack of cards – hearts, diamonds, clubs and spades – were first devised in France in the fifteenth century. The French call diamonds 'tiles', clubs 'clovers' and spades 'pikes'.

The Fantastic Facts (all the Rest are Fab Fibs!)

HOW TO MAKE YOUR BIKE SOUND LIKE A MOTORBIKE

Fantastic Fact

The fastest man on a bicycle has pedalled himself up to a speed of more than 269 kph (167 mph). He was a Dutch cyclist called Fred Rompelberg and he pedalled behind a drag racing car on the Bonneville Salt Flats in the United States in 1995.

They didn't have paratroops during the First World War and even if they did, whoever heard of an edible bicycle? Get real! And Catchimifyoucan was a bit of a giveaway for the Aztec cyclists, wasn't it? (Catch-im-if-you-can.)

HOW TO GET OUT OF KISSING YOUR AUNTIE
Fantastic Fact
The muscle you use to pucker your lips for a kiss is called the orbicularis oris. It just is. That's a biological fact. Hopefully, none of you were fooled by the toe curling nonsense or the stuff about the Frankfurt teenagers.

HOW TO GET OUT OF EATING SPROUTS
Fantastic Fact

I was expecting something a bit bigger...

Brussels sprouts are traditionally grown in Belgium, taking their name from the capital of the country, but were almost certainly first cultivated in ancient Rome. That's so obviously true that it probably looked like it had to be a lie. If you were caught out by the double bluff, you should be ashamed of yourself. Since when can peas make you deaf? Never! And the Federation Internationale de Boiling is shortened to, of course, FIB!

HOW TO WIN AT NOUGHTS AND CROSSES
Fantastic Fact
Archaeologists excavating in Rome have uncovered long-lost noughts and crosses grids chalked or scratched on ancient stonework – all true AND... The maximum number of 'X's (or

'O's) that you can fit on a noughts and crosses board without having three in a row is six – also true! Try it some time. You use opposite corners and the adjacent squares, but not the middle. You didn't fall for the soldier story, did you?

HOW TO WATCH TELLY PAST YOUR BEDTIME
Fantastic Fact
Even Simon Cowell wasn't around as long ago as 1876 and you can't boost the batteries in the remote with your brain, otherwise no one would ever buy new batteries, would they? But 20 million viewers in Britain did watch Queen Elizabeth II's coronation in 1953 and people watched with whomever they knew who actually had a telly.

HOW TO GET OUT OF LISTENING TO YOUR PARENTS' MUSIC IN THE CAR
Fantastic Fact
In 1979, singer Gary Numan released a single called 'Cars', the lyrics of which were written after he experienced a road rage incident. It was a big hit, so that's a fact.

Car tyres do have metal strips in them but they are for strength and nothing to do with radio reception. There are some strange laws in America, but those mentioned are totally bogus.

HOW TO GET OUT OF SITTING IN THE MIDDLE
Fantastic Fact
The first car manufacturer to fit modern seat belts to a car as standard equipment was the Swedish company Volvo in 1959. Volvos are famous for being safe cars, and that's a fact.

Your sense of smell won't actually force you to hate someone, even if they smell like a rotting dungheap, and you'd be very unlucky to have a rat make its home in the back seat of your car.

HOW TO GET YOUR DOG ACTUALLY TO EAT YOUR HOMEWORK
Fantastic Fact
As far as scientists have been able to discover, nothing travels faster than the speed of light. Light travels at more than 186,000 miles per second. To give some idea of how fast that is, the circumference of the Earth is about 25,000 miles and light could, therefore, travel right around the world more than seven times in just one second. That is true... AND... The tallest dog ever was called Giant George, a Great Dane who was more than two metres (seven feet) tall when he stood on his hind legs and who became so famous that he appeared on *The Oprah Winfrey Show* on TV. Also true – Giant George was on Oprah. Lucky Reggazoni, on the other wet hand, never existed.

HOW TO GET OUT OF GARDENING

Fantastic Fact

The Hanging Gardens of Babylon are famously known as one of the original Seven Wonders of the World, but no one knows exactly where they might have been. They may have been in the ancient city of Babylon (now Hillah in Iraq) or could possibly have been in Mosul, about four hundred and two kilometres (two hundred and fifty miles) north of Baghdad in Iraq.

HOW TO GET YOUR PARENTS TO GIVE YOU DOUBLE POCKET MONEY

Fantastic Fact

In 2002, the euro took over completely from a whole load of European currencies, making the mark, franc, lira, escudo and schilling no longer legal tender. That actually happened, but 'dosh' doesn't mean 'dollars or silver handy.' Some think it may be a combination of 'dollars' and 'cash', but there are many other ideas about where the term may have come from. Try looking it up in a dictionary or online. Thomas Crapper did manufacture toilets, but he did not invent the first flushing toilet.

HOW TO MAKE SOMEBODY DO A CHICKEN IMPRESSION

Fantastic Fact

In Arizona, in America in the 1940s, a chicken called Mike lived for one and a half years after his head had been cut off. It's

145

almost unbelievable, but it is true. Food and water were given to him through his neck. Weird and spooky.

It is also a fact that if you tell a lie in a court of law, after having sworn to tell the truth, you are committing a crime called perjury and can be prosecuted. But nobody ever lived as a seal in London Zoo

HOW TO SNEAK DOWNSTAIRS WITHOUT WAKING YOUR PARENTS
Fantastic Fact
Melvyn Switzer from Kent, England, snored so loudly that he set a world record. He snored at ninety-two decibels, which was louder than having a truck driving through the room, but not quite as dangerous. You'd have to have been hypnotised yourself to believe that story about the cinema usher in Milan but there's a bit more truth to the fib about the bones in the ear. The hammer, anvil and stirrup really are small bones that transmit sound wave vibrations. The flange, the grommet, the biscuit and the plin are made up. You do grow while you sleep, but you don't actively shrink if you don't get eight hours per night.

HOW TO GET OUT OF EATING FOREIGN MUCK ON HOLIDAY
Fantastic Fact
The Greek writer Homer, born around 2,700 years ago, wrote about a kind of sausage in his epic poem *The Odyssey*. Unlikely as it might seem, a sausage really did appear in *The Odyssey* –

'a sizzling sausage' it said, 'packed with fat and blood.' Sounds like a black pudding, actually, but that's still a sausage, so that's still a fact ... AND ... more than 50 per cent of raw chicken contains bacteria that cause more illnesses than salmonella – nasty but true. Chicken has to be cooked properly to kill off those bugs. Fish, on the other hand, or foot, don't have fingers, or toes.

HOW TO CONVINCE YOUR YOUNGER SIBLING THEIR ROOM IS HAUNTED

Fantastic Fact

The White House in Washington, home to the President of the United States, is said to be haunted by several ghosts, including Abigail Adams (wife of the country's second President, John Adams), former President Abraham Lincoln and a certain Mr Burns, who once owned the land on which the White House is built. All true. There is no truth, however, in the idea that dogs or cats leave the room when a ghost comes in, although you can have some fun spooking your brother or sister with that big, fat fib. Toulouse Lautrec was famously short, but kicking people in the shins under the table? Don't say you thought it might be true!

HOW TO GET OUT OF SITTING NEXT TO THE NUTTER ON THE BUS

Fantastic Fact

Queue (the kind you stand in waiting at a bus stop) and cue (the kind that men in fancy waistcoats use to play snooker) may be spelt differently but they sound the same. Such words are called homophones. Another useful fact, even if it does sound like something you might have learned by chance in the classroom when you were accidentally paying attention for once. The three-wheeled bus is about as likely as a three-legged hippie, and if falling asleep on the bus was a criminal offence anywhere, they'd need a lot more prisons!

HOW TO WIN AT ROCK, PAPER, SCISSORS

Fantastic Fact

Because the Chinese invented paper, you might think that rock, paper, scissors was first played in China, and you would be right – although it was played as 'slug, frog, snake'. It's true, and so is the fact that paper is the least popular move in a game of rock, paper, scissors. Studies have shown that it is used around 30 per cent of the time while rock and scissors are each used around 35 per cent each. Maybe Jacques l'Esparrow (Jack Sparrow) gave you a clue that the marathon game was a hoax.

HOW TO GET OUT OF GAMES AND PE
Fantastic Fact

There are more than 100 countries in the official Rugby Union world rankings, including Uzbekistan at number 96 and New Zealand at number 1. The first Rugby World Cup was won by New Zealand in 1987. That is true, although the world rankings may have changed slightly by the time you are reading this.

The player credited with inventing rugby by catching a football and running with it during a game was actually William Webb Ellis, not Henry, and he went, of course, to Rugby School, not Eton. Playing sports doesn't necessarily make some people annoying, and there has been no research at Lancaster or anywhere else to prove it.

HOW TO MAKE IT LOOK LIKE YOU'VE HAD A SHOWER AT SCHOOL WITHOUT ACTUALLY HAVING HAD ONE
Fantastic Fact

Having a shower is more eco-friendly than taking a bath because it uses less water. A shower may use between forty-five to ninety litres (ten and twenty gallons) of water, where a bath can use more than three times that amount – completely true. AND... At New York State University in Buffalo, Kevin 'Catfish' McCartney set a record for the longest ever shower, staying under the shower head for over 340 hours – that's more than two weeks! Also completely true. Catfish must have been the cleanest student ever. There is no truth, however, in the idea that taking a shower can give you brain damage.

HOW TO GET OUT OF BEING BLAMED FOR A FART ON A PLANE
Fantastic Fact

On average, a person (male or female) produces half a litre of fart gas (0.8) every day. On a four-hour flight in a plane carrying 500 people, the air conditioning has to clear over forty litres (seventy pints) of farts. Disturbingly, this is basically true. If you caught all the farts in a big bag, it would need a seat all to itself, and who would want to sit next to it? At the time of writing, no one from Kirkcaldy has managed to run a motorbike on his own farts, but on reading this someone is bound to try. And the dolphins – fairly obviously a fib, isn't it?

HOW TO WIN AN ARGUMENT WITH YOUR SISTER OR BROTHER
Fantastic Fact

The four 'suits' in a standard pack of cards – hearts, diamonds, clubs and spades – were first devised in France in the fifteenth century. The French call diamonds 'tiles', clubs 'clovers' and spades 'pikes'. All of that is true, but Harold and Margaret Evans are totally fictitious and if you add together the numbers on all of the cards in a pack, counting the ace as 1 and face cards as 10, the total is not 365. It comes close, though... work it out for yourself.